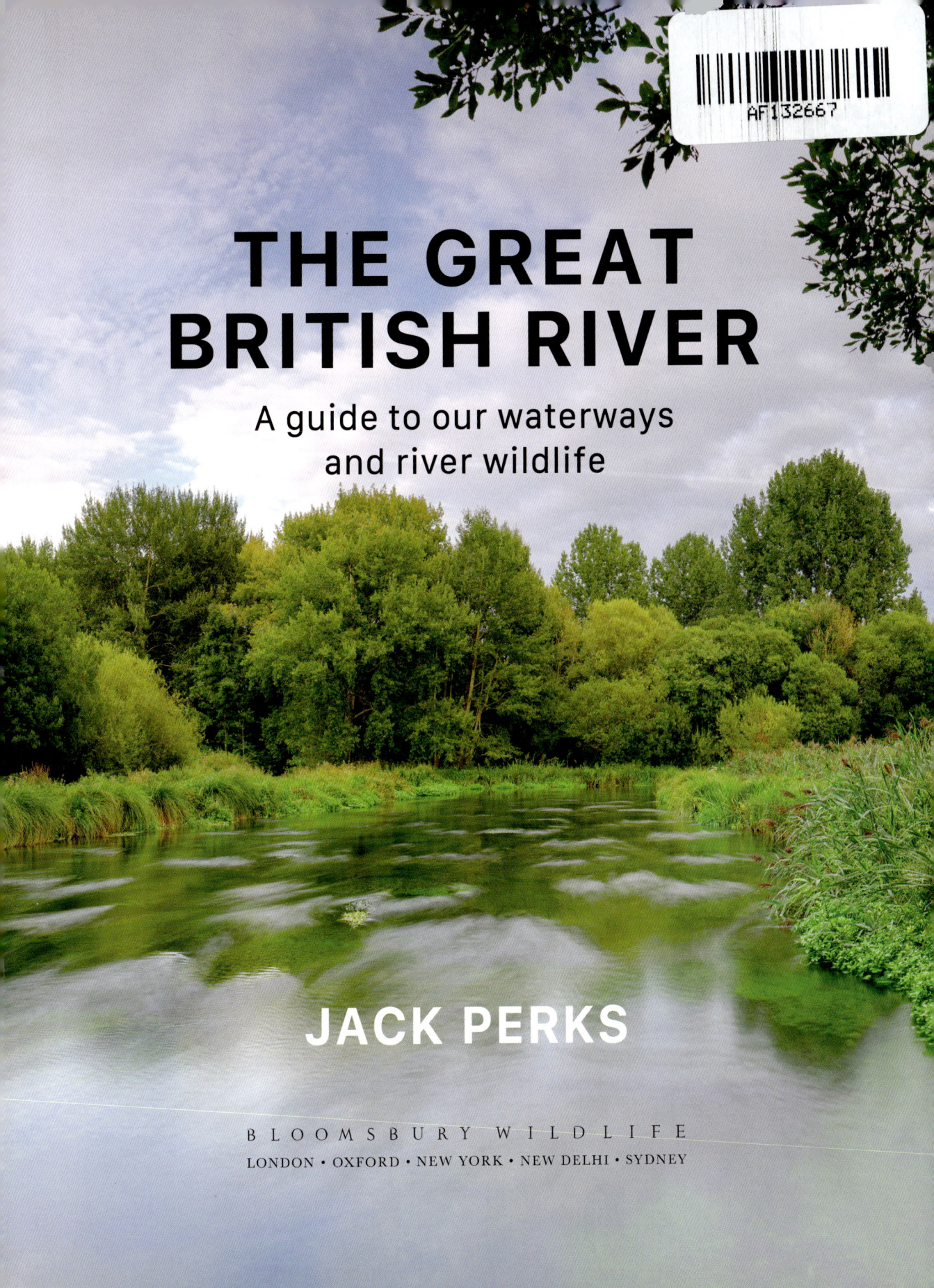

THE GREAT BRITISH RIVER

A guide to our waterways
and river wildlife

JACK PERKS

BLOOMSBURY WILDLIFE
LONDON · OXFORD · NEW YORK · NEW DELHI · SYDNEY

BLOOMSBURY WILDLIFE
Bloomsbury Publishing Plc
50 Bedford Square, London, WC1B 3DP, UK
Bloomsbury Publishing Ireland Limited,
29 Earlsfort Terrace, Dublin 2, D02 AY28, Ireland

BLOOMSBURY, BLOOMSBURY WILDLIFE and the Diana logo are trademarks of Bloomsbury Publishing Plc

First published in the United Kingdom 2026

Copyright © Jack Perks, 2026

Jack Perks has asserted his right under the Copyright, Designs and Patents Act, 1988, to be identified as Author of this work

For legal purposes the Acknowledgements on p. 174 constitute an extension of this copyright page

All rights reserved. No part of this publication may be: i) reproduced or transmitted in any form, electronic or mechanical, including photocopying, recording or by means of any information storage or retrieval system without prior permission in writing from the publishers; or ii) used or reproduced in any way for the training, development or operation of artificial intelligence (AI) technologies, including generative AI technologies. The rights holders expressly reserve this publication from the text and data mining exception as per Article 4(3) of the Digital Single Market Directive (EU) 2019/790

Bloomsbury Publishing Plc does not have any control over, or responsibility for, any third-party websites referred to or in this book. All internet addresses given in this book were correct at the time of going to press. The author and publisher regret any inconvenience caused if addresses have changed or sites have ceased to exist, but can accept no responsibility for any such changes

A catalogue record for this book is available from the British Library

Library of Congress Cataloguing-in-Publication data has been applied for

ISBN: PB: 9781-3994-1398-5; ePub: 978-1-3994-1400-5; ePDF: 978-1-3994-1397-8

10 9 8 7 6 5 4 3 2 1

Typeset in IvyStyle Sans
Designed by Austin Taylor
Printed and bound in China by RR Donnelley Asia Printing Solutions Ltd

To find out more about our authors and books visit www.bloomsbury.com and sign up for our newsletters
For product safety related questions contact productsafety@bloomsbury.com

Title: River Itchen near Martyr Worthy, Hampshire.
This spread: River Wye, Ross-on-Wye, Herefordshire.

Contents

Introduction 4

1 The Source 8

2 Upper Reaches 24

3 Middle Reaches 40

4 Lower Reaches 56

5 The Estuary 72

6 Chalk Streams 88

7 Canals 104

8 Urban Rivers 120

9 Scottish Spate Rivers 136

10 Ponds 152

River Pubs 168 | River Names 170

Glossary 172 | Organisations 173

Acknowledgements 174 | Photo Credits 174

Index 175

Introduction

Great Britain is a land of many rivers, which, with their dynamic landscapes, are crucial for wildlife and people. Put very simply, a river is a body of flowing water that, in most cases, will eventually snake its way towards the sea. But rivers are, in reality, complex systems of interconnecting habitats, from upland moors down to salt marshes. They are the arteries of the country. As well as providing animals with fresh water to drink, rivers provide a home for many specialist aquatic species, which in turn feed other species, such as birds that feast on river fly hatches or deer that graze on bankside vegetation.

How many rivers in Britain?

The exact number of rivers in Britain is debatable but, according to the National River Flow Archive, there are estimated to be 1,500 discrete river systems with more than 125,000 miles of riverbank across the UK as a whole. Although this seems like a lot, from a global perspective our rivers are relatively short, shallow and heavily influenced by human actions.

Around 20,000 years ago Britain was connected to Europe via a stretch of land called Doggerland, where the North Sea is now. This low-lying area would have been flat and full of wetlands, resembling modern-day Norfolk or the Netherlands. Britain's and Europe's rivers were connected, with the Thames joining the Rhine to flow into the English Channel. However, melting ice caps caused a huge flood, which drowned Doggerland and cut Britain off from the rest of Europe. This event drastically shortened many rivers that had previously flowed into Doggerland.

Many of our rivers have formed their course over millions of years. Some form from underground springs and aquifers, like the famous chalk streams of Wessex and Norfolk, while others flow from mountain snowmelt collecting in the lower ground. Most rivers start at a higher point and work their way to lower ground. Rivers will often join and lead into other rivers, so we tend

↑ Brown trout, River Frome, Dorset.

to mark the start of a river at the source and the end of that particular river when it reaches another river or the sea. For example the Derbyshire Derwent enters the River Trent at Derwent Mouth near Sawley where they merge. When you have multiple rivers, streams and brooks that are all connected this is known as the catchment, and there are multiple catchments across the country.

Changing rivers

Each year our rivers are changed by floods, erosion and, in many cases, humans altering their course. Under this constant pressure, rivers are vulnerable habitats. Rivers have been vital to human progress over the ages, from our extracting drinking water to utilising their flow to provide power and transport. The Romans, around 2,000 years ago, started to drain low-lying areas such as the Somerset Levels and the Fens, and used the reclaimed land for farming and settlements, creating artificial flood defences in order to control the tides. These defences were composed of ditches, dug to create a network of channels that would drain the marshland. The Romans also dug the very first canals in Britain, connecting water bodies previously closed off to each other. These flood defences didn't last long, however, as once the Romans left Britain they were no longer maintained. It wasn't until the seventeenth century that these areas were fully drained and engineered for farming. With the rise of industry and factories up until the early twentieth century, rivers were used as highways for goods and the disposal of waste. More canals were built and rivers were straightened to suit our transport needs.

The state of our rivers

At the time of writing, Britain's rivers are in a very poor state, which is putting it mildly. During the industrial revolution in the nineteenth century, many rivers were essentially open sewers, with rising populations and industry dumping untreated human waste and chemicals straight into them. The River Don in Sheffield once held the title of the most polluted river in Europe, sometimes stained a bright orange from the many heavy metals dumped into it.

Over the next hundred years, rivers were improved, with better sewage filtration as people became more aware of the side effects of the pollutants going into the river. Species such as otters and salmon returned to rivers where they had long been absent. The phrase 'Britain's rivers have never been cleaner' was routinely quoted by various press and government outlets. Now, in the 2020s, this phrase has all but died out and the scales have started to tip the other way again. While our rivers are nowhere near as bad as they were in the nineteenth century, they are becoming worse in many respects, with sewage routinely dumped, excessive abstraction, agricultural runoff and human-made barriers to migration for fish such as salmon, shad and lamprey. It's causing a sort of death by a thousand cuts and we are starting to see the gravity of the situation.

Today, under the EU Water Framework Directive, only 14 per cent of English rivers are classified as being in good ecological health, and none are classified as being in good chemical health or good overall health. The Environment Agency reported 3.6 million hours of sewage spills in 2023, and the problem is seemingly getting worse. According to the charity WildFish, more than 350,000 regulated chemicals are in use in Great Britain, but our rivers are only checked for 52 of them. Sadly, there seems to be a distinct lack of interest from government to hold to account those who are destroying British rivers.

It can seem like a losing battle, but rivers are a precious resource that need defending. In November 2024, more than 15,000 people marched on Westminster to protest the appalling state of our rivers. Many organisations have voiced their concerns, with groups such as Fish Legal and WildFish taking the government to court for inadequate action on upholding river quality. The plight of rivers is now squarely in the public eye and pressure to improve them is mounting. By collectively fighting for our rivers, we can try to turn things around.

Celebrating our rivers

Even though many rivers are in trouble, we can still enjoy them and the amazing scenery, wildlife and activities that many of them have to offer.

It sounds very clichéd, but for as long as I can remember I've had an interest in nature and an almost magnetic draw towards running water. There would always be a bullhead (a small bottom-dwelling fish) to find under a rock or a frog jumping out of the long grass. I grew up on a large council estate in Nottingham, so not an especially green place, but a small river nearby, Fairham Brook, was my escape. My grandad would take me to watch the Sunday league football, but I'd always sneak off to see the shoal of chub under the willow tree. Somehow, and I'm still not entirely sure how, I've turned this fascination into a full-time career filming British wildlife underwater, and for the last decade I have jumped into just about every river in Britain.

There are many kinds of river, and throughout this book we'll explore some of the different types, and the habitats they supply, starting at the source where a river begins and working our way downstream to where the river meets the sea at the estuary. Each type of river and each section along it has its own unique cast of characters, from house martins making their homes in walls along urban rivers to salmon pushing upstream in the fast flows of Scottish spate rivers.

Rivers are places that offer many of us valuable time in nature, away from our busy lives, whether we're fishing, walking, boating, swimming or enjoying one of the many other activities a river has to offer. If we are lucky, we may see some of the many creatures that make their homes in and around rivers. Throughout this guide, we'll journey along some of our most beautiful and vital rivers, meet some of the species that depend on them, and discover ways we can enjoy our local rivers and how we can help to protect them. The river is a natural pathway to follow and we all have that little bit of curiosity as to what's around the next bend.

↓ Carrbridge Packhorse Bridge, Scottish Highlands.

→ Map showing a selection of British rivers.

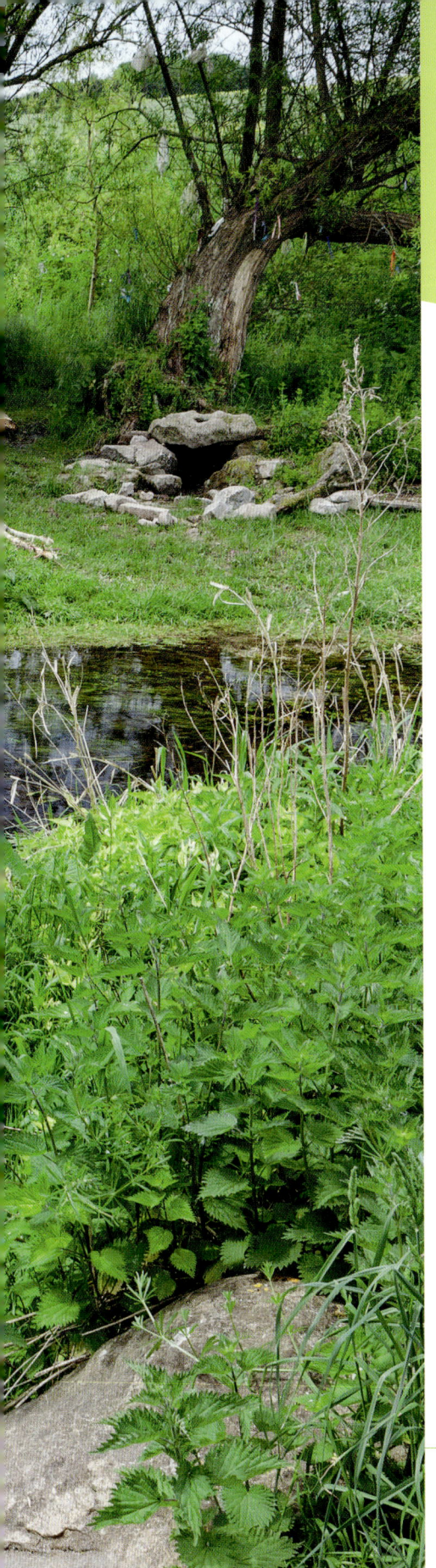

1

The Source

The source is where a river begins. The type of source varies from river to river, from a small underground spring to a large mountain lake, but it will typically be located on higher ground, such as a mountain or hill. The water at the source, known as headwaters, is usually the cleanest of any point of the river, as it is yet to be polluted by human interaction. Because of this clean water, the source is often a last refuge for species that require highly oxygenated water, such as river flies (insects with aquatic larvae, including mayflies, stoneflies and caddisflies), white-clawed crayfish and lampreys, which can all eke out a living in the shallow, gravelly water.

There's an almost spiritual significance to the birth of a river and you can really get a sense of this when you see clean pure water appear out of the ground or from a hillside above you.

← One of the springs at the source of the River Kennet in Wiltshire.

Where do rivers start?

It can sometimes be hard to determine the actual source and starting point of a river, as some rivers have multiple starting points that all converge into one main water body. Generally you go to the point furthest away from the estuary (the end of the river) but this can be up for debate: if you have multiple arms all joining one main river then which is the actual 'start'? There isn't really a definitive answer for this.

Climate plays a huge part in where a river starts. Warming temperatures are melting snowy headwaters more quickly, meaning less water is ending up in upland rivers with it all dumped into the system quickly rather than in a gradual release. Many of the species that live in this fast-flowing and cool water rely on its lower temperatures, therefore warming waters mean many of these species end up without suitable habitat. Being aquatic, they will struggle to recolonise elsewhere after they have been wiped out in a particular river. These higher colder areas are an ark site providing a safe haven for many river flies (of which the larvae are aquatic), trout and molluscs.

GLACIAL MELT

Some British rivers are glacially fed; these are mostly found in the Lake District, North Wales and the highlands of Scotland. These rivers start life at the top of mountains where it's cooler and ice slowly melts. In a natural cycle, this is a slow release of water and it will refreeze in the winter with snow and rain replenishing it.

However, rising temperatures cause the ice to melt more rapidly, without being topped up. This means a higher volume of water is discharged in a shorter amount of time while, in the long run, less water is fed from higher elevations with higher temperatures, leading to less snow.

↓ The River Liza flows through a glacial valley in Ennerdale, Cumbria.

AQUIFERS

In essence, an aquifer is a body of porous rock or sediment saturated with groundwater. Water enters an aquifer when precipitation seeps through the soil. It moves through the aquifer and resurfaces through springs and wells. This type of river source is most commonly associated with chalk streams, as the chalk is a perfect medium for this process, but it does also occur in limestone rivers. Temperature and climate are again significant in the role of an aquifer as the starting point of a river. You need a steady amount of rain to recharge these aquifers so that they can slowly release the water to get the river started. If there are prolonged dry periods, whole stretches of river can completely dry up.

FIELDS OF MOSS

The source of many rivers is found in the uplands, where these first trickles of water are surrounded by mossy bogs and a peaty landscape. This huge expanse of bog plays a vital role in stabilising the climate, as it acts as a carbon trap.

It may not look glamorous, but sphagnum moss, the moss growing within most peat bogs, is a crucial part of upland habitat. Most people think of moss as being green but sphagnum comes in a range of colours, from yellow to brown and red, and more than 25 species of sphagnum moss can be found across the British Isles. Carpeting the moorlands, it acts as a giant sponge which can absorb up to 20 times its own weight in water, holding it in special empty cells within its structure. During heavy rain, water is held back and released slowly, alleviating floods downstream and allowing water to be distributed over time.

Sphagnum moss is an important component in the formation of peat, which is the result of incomplete decomposition of the remains of moss and other plants growing in waterlogged conditions. Peatlands only cover about 12 percent of the land surface in the UK, but store as much carbon as the forests of the UK, France and Germany combined.

As well as stopping flooding and storing carbon, sphagnum moss is an important habitat for many specialist moorland creatures. Sundews

↑ Moss is an important part of the upland ecosystem.

are predatory plants that like to root themselves amongst the moss and wait for small insects to fall into the plant's 'mouth'. Many springtails, harvestmen and woodlice call these damp and dark crevices home.

Which is the main river?

It can get a little confusing when you have multiple rivers all joining and mixing into one. As a rule of thumb, the river with the longest course downstream of the source is considered the 'main' river and the other, smaller rivers leading into it are considered tributaries. For example, the Thames is the main river as it is the longest, but many smaller rivers join it along the way, such as the Lea and the Wandle. Even though these rivers may have different names, they are still all connected in what is known as a catchment. In Britain, it's thought that we have about 130 distinct catchments, though some are artificially linked via canals and ditches.

The perils of flea treatments

Thirty-six per cent of British people own dogs, and man's best friend often joins us on our riverside walks. This can bring them into contact with parasites such as fleas, ticks and flies. As these can cause the dogs some distress, many owners naturally want to protect their pets by using flea treatment. However, this can have some unintended effects on the wider environment. New analysis of Environment Agency data by the Rivers Trust and the Wildlife and Countryside Link shows that three insecticides used widely in tick, flea and worm treatments (fipronil, permethrin and the controversial neonicotinoid imidacloprid) are present in English rivers in concentrations that exceed accepted safe limits for wildlife. This is despite the fact that these chemicals are deemed too toxic to be used in agriculture. The issue is that these insecticides do not solely kill parasites, but all invertebrates, so many species of mayfly, dragonfly and shrimp are hit hard by this new threat to river wildlife. To give you an idea of how potent some of these chemicals are, imidacloprid, if used in a single flea treatment of a medium-sized dog, can contain enough pesticide to kill 60 million bees. The chemicals find their way into rivers by two methods: one is by dogs swimming in pond and river water and the second is from owners washing their hands after applying the treatment (so cat owners aren't off the hook either!).

Until these chemicals are banned, the best pest control methods to avoid any harm to our river-dwelling invertebrates are regular grooming to remove flea eggs and ticks, and the use of herbal shampoos and a natural flea collar.

Stepping stones

Many rivers in Britain have stepping stones, which are a favourite among walkers. These are large flat stones that have been deliberately placed in the river to allow passage across without getting too wet. They tend to be found higher up a river where the water is shallower. It means there's no need for a bridge, and the stones fit into the environment nicely. In quieter areas, they even provide perches for many birds, such as goosander, grey wagtails and, of course, dippers. While stepping stones are not exclusive to the Peak District, this region does hold some of the better-known ones. For example, Dovedale's stepping stones are an easy walk from

↑ Keeping dogs on the lead by rivers helps to stop flea treatments from entering the water system.

→ Chee Dale Stepping Stones, Peak District.

the car park, and there are also the Bamford Mill stepping stones, which are a bit more elevated. Decent footwear is advised as the stones can be slippery, and a long stick can be useful to help steady yourself.

River dipping

While pond dipping is a more well-known pastime, river dipping can reveal a whole range of rewarding species like stone loach, mayfly larvae and bullheads, which are not found in still waters. In principle, the technique for river dipping is the same as for pond dipping: use a net to sweep in the margins and see what can be collected.

One of the most common methods of river dipping is a survey technique called 'kick sampling', where you stand in the river and carefully move the riverbed with your foot to disturb what's living in there, placing the net behind your foot so the flow washes anything into it. This is a great way to find river fly larvae, which are normally quite elusive, and get an idea of river health and quality as the river flies need high water quality to thrive.

Not all rivers are suitable for river dipping, and of course you need to be careful near strong flows, deep water and slippery banks. The source of a river is often narrow and shallow, so an ideal place to river dip. It's often best to start either from the margins or in shallow gravelly water. You can use the end of your net to check how firm the riverbed is, as it can sometimes look shallow but be full of silt – a hard gravel bottom is easiest to stand on.

RIVER DIPPING TIPS

- **Think about what you'd like to find and choose your net accordingly.** You can get different nets with different-sized holes. If it's smaller invertebrates you're looking for, then a smaller mesh net is better. If it's small fish you're after, then a larger mesh will help filter out debris and keep the fish in.
- **Make sure you have a small white tray** to empty what you catch onto so you can spot the smaller species more easily. A small transparent tank is also ideal for getting a closer look at what you've caught.
- Remember to **return what you catch** as close as possible to where you caught it.
- **Make sure you have wellies** if you want to enter shallow water, or footwear with good grip.
- If you've never done any kind of dipping before, I suggest **trying a small pond first!**

→ The River Windrush, in Bourton-on-the-Water in the Cotswolds, is a popular spot for walkers.

Riverside walks

There's something meditative about walking alongside water, and the river, being a path of sorts, is many walkers' favourite choice. Many of us may enjoy a walk near a river as part of our daily lives, with the walk to work or school taking us along its banks, while others may be more proactive and plan a weekend riverside walk. Two of the obvious benefits are the exercise, getting the blood pumping and legs moving, and the excitement of not knowing what's going to be around the next bend – perhaps a cascading riffle or an electric blue flash of a kingfisher.

Another huge benefit of a riverside walk is the boost it can give our mental health. The act of walking concentrates the mind on a simple task, often helping to clear our head of negative thoughts.

We know through studies that people visit lakes and the sea on a more seasonal basis, tending to go in the summer, while rivers seem to hold our interest year-round. Maybe the stronger flows in the winter draw us in.

The riverside is also a sensory explosion: the smell of flowering riverside plants in the summer; the sound of a grey wagtail calling on the far bank; and the touch of the cool water on your feet on a hot day all add to the experience and help to lift the mood. Whether you take your own route or follow a designated path, there's plenty of choice for riverside walks and the source of a river is an excellent starting point.

Throughout the book, I suggest a few riverside walks that you may want to try out, from accessible walks in city centres to rugged uphill walks in the Scottish uplands.

MAKING THE MOST OF YOUR WALK

- The old saying 'There's no bad weather, just the wrong clothing' is something I firmly believe in. Riversides are often muddy so thick **walking boots and waterproof trousers are a must!**
- **I always have my phone on me, which acts as a back-up camera.** If you have binoculars, you can press the phone camera up to them to create a makeshift long lens, which is useful for getting shots of shy animals.
- While the walk is the objective for many of us, it's also important to just be in the moment. I often like to **just sit in one spot for a while** and really take everything in.
- **Plan a route:** work out what you want to see, how far to go and where the end destination is – for me, normally a country pub and a pint! (I've listed some of my favourites on page 168.)

Where to visit

RIVER THAMES, Kemble

Old Father Thames is perhaps the most well-known British river internationally, thanks to its looming presence through the capital, but it has a very humble start near Kemble in the Cotswolds, 110m above sea level. Known as Thames Head, the source is seasonal so, depending on when you go, there might not actually be any water. For the best chance of seeing the source, go in the winter or after heavy rain.

As with many other rivers, there is debate as to whether this is in fact the true source, but most people are in agreement that Thames Head is the start of the Thames. There is a marker stone where one of the springs comes out to showcase the start of the river.

The surrounding area is a mixture of pasture, farmland and grassland with a host of wildflowers and bird species such as yellowhammer, greenfinch and skylark.

It's an easy walk to Thames Head from Kemble at just under three miles on fairly level ground, though it can be muddy in the winter. If you fancy a longer walk, this is also the start of the Thames Path, which, at 184 miles along the banks of the River Thames, is the longest designated river path in Europe. The Thames is the second-longest river in Britain (after the Severn) at 215 miles long and technically the longest river that continually flows in England, as part of the Severn is in Wales. The Thames ends its course at Southend-on-Sea and has many tributaries including the Coln, Churn, Evenlode, Kennet, Lea, Leach, Loddon, Ock and Windrush. More than 200 bridges cross the Thames, with 20 of them being in Central London, and it is tidal up to Teddington.

The name 'Thames' is thought to mean 'dark' or 'mud' in Britannic, and of course its lower reaches are quite murky.

RIVER TRENT, Biddulph Moor

Located in the Staffordshire moorlands, the source of the River Trent, also known as Trent Head Well, can be found just outside the village of Biddulph, 300m above sea level. Having grown up in Nottingham, I always find it very strange to think there are parts of the Trent you can jump across, as my local stretch is wider than a football pitch.

To see the source, it's a short walk of less than half a mile from Biddulph village down a public footpath. The surrounding moorland is home to many birds, including short-eared owl, hobby and red grouse as well as insects such as emperor moth and pearl-bordered fritillary butterfly.

There are many other walking routes along the Trent, including the Trent Valley Way, which covers 154 miles from Rugeley to Alkborough. There are also smaller routes that take you around Biddulph Moor, and even a route from Stoke-on-Trent to the source, which is roughly three hours long and about nine miles in length.

The Trent is the third-longest river in Britain, at 185 miles long, passing through Burton-on-Trent, Stoke-on-Trent and Nottingham before meeting the Ouse and becoming the Humber at Trent Falls in Lincolnshire. The name 'Trent' is likely from a Romano-British word meaning 'strongly flooding', as much of its course is in low-lying ground with surrounding floodplains. Historically, the Trent was the border between the north and south of England (though personally I've always classed myself as an East Midlander). It's highly unusual in that it is the only river in Great Britain that flows north. Once it gets to Newark, it bends around and heads north towards the Humber. The river has many tributaries including the Mease, Dove, Soar, Derwent, Idle, Blithe and Fairham Brook. Half of the Trent is tidal, up to Cromwell Weir in Nottinghamshire. There are nine major weirs and barriers, which allow some degree of passage for migratory fish, but more work is needed to improve fish movement.

RIVER SEVERN, Plynlimon

The longest river in Britain, at 220 miles, the River Severn starts in mid Wales in the Cambrian Mountains, over 600m above sea level. Unlike the Thames and the Trent, it's hard to say exactly where the start of the Severn is, as the area is one huge peat bog, which acts like a huge sponge collecting rainwater and moisture – of which there is a lot! As it's only 15 miles from the Welsh coast, the moist sea air hits the hills and regularly condenses as rain.

The area is walkable, with an incline as you might expect, and is the highest part of the Severn Way walking route, which is 214 miles long in total. In the hills around Plynlimon, you can still find good numbers of hen harrier, merlin and black grouse, as well as plenty of plant life, including dwarf bilberry, crowberry, mosses and clubmosses. You'll see a stone pillar marking the approximate source of the Severn. Start at Hafren Forest car park, where you can pick up the Severn Way and follow the waymarked trail north-west.

When you think of the River Severn you might not immediately think of waterfalls, but it does indeed boast some higher up the catchment. One is known as 'Severn Break its Neck', which is easily accessible via a trail just outside of Llanidloes town centre in Powys, with parking nearby at the Rhyd-y-benwch car park. While walking on this route, you'll find many cascades and plunge pools that are formed as a result of the Severn carving its path through the forest.

The River Severn gets its name from the Latin word 'Sabrina', named by the Romans. This was eventually Anglicized to become Severn. The Welsh name for 'Sabrina' is 'Hafren' and when translated to English means 'boundary'. The Severn has many tributaries but its major ones are the Vyrnwy, the Tern, the Teme, the Warwickshire Avon and the Worcestershire Stour. The river ends its journey at the Bristol Channel.

RIVER CLYDE, Lowther Hills

The Clyde is one of Scotland's most historically important rivers in terms of industrialisation. Flowing through the centre of Glasgow, the river was instrumental to the shipbuilding industry of the area in the nineteenth century. Everything from cruise liners to warships were made here. Rising in the Lowther Hills of Lanarkshire, the confluence of two streams, the Daer Water and Potrail Water, is widely considered to be the start of the Clyde. The Lowther Hills are 725m above sea level and are rich in natural minerals, with a couple of villages set up to take advantage of this. In fact, these are the highest villages in Scotland. The area became known as 'God's Treasure House' as it has produced some of the world's purest gold (22.8 carats), which was used in the manufacture of the Scottish Crown Jewels. Lead was also mined extensively from the thirteenth century onwards and gave the area its other name: the Lead Hills.

Glenochar is the closest village to the source, with roadside parking from which you can walk across a field to see the start of the Clyde. The hillside is dominated by dwarf shrubs, principally common heather, bell heather and cross-leaved heath but also includes rare plants such as lesser twayblade orchid. The heath is managed for grouse shooting, with burnings happening periodically, and as well as the red grouse the moorland is home to some specialist insects such as bilberry bumblebee, heather fly and northern eggar, a large moth in which the males are day-flying but the females are nocturnal.

The Clyde runs at a length of 106 miles and eventually meets the Firth of Clyde, mixing with the North Sea. The Clyde has many tributaries including the Leven, Kelvin and Nethan, the Black Cart Water, White Cart Water, the Avon Water, the North Calder Water and the South Calder Water.

Species spotlight

CASTOR BEAN TICK *Ixodes ricinus*

We have 20 species of tick in Great Britain, most of which are highly specialised to a particular host, such as the hedgehog tick or the ornate cow tick. However, the most common is the castor bean tick, which is often found on cats, dogs and even people. The name comes from its resemblance to the castor bean. They can be tiny, with unfed nymphs around 1.3mm, but a well-fed female can swell up to 11mm.

They like humid environments so the banks of small rivers are ideal, with plenty of animals passing by for a drink. Due to milder winters, ticks are spreading and expanding their range and are now active throughout the year.

Ticks are well known for carrying a myriad of diseases, including Lyme disease, which often reveals itself with a red 'bullseye' mark around the area of the bite. If you experience any symptoms of a cold after a tick bite, it's best to get checked by a GP.

When walking in areas with a high likelihood of ticks, wear long trousers tucked into socks and apply repellent. If you find one on your skin, remove it with a tick remover to avoid leaving the serrated mouth parts in.

PALMATE NEWT *Lissotriton helveticus*

On harsh open moorlands, the streams trickling along often create small boggy ponds. The ponds normally have a high acid content, which limits what can live in them, but one amphibian thrives here: the palmate newt.

It is not a rare species by any means, but it does tend to do far better when not competing with the more common smooth newt or its larger cousin, the great crested newt. Unlike other newts, it can be found in slow-running water, using upland streams as pathways to new water bodies.

Palmate newts get their name from the webbed hind feet that the males develop during the breeding season, along with a thin tippet at the end of the tail to help attract a female. The body is a pale brown colour, with a creamy underbelly. Unlike the other native newt species, the male doesn't have a crest and both sexes generally have few, if any, spots on the belly. The smallest newt species in Britain, they tend to reach sizes of 8cm.

As with all British newts, the male will drop a packet of sperm for the female to manoeuvre over and suck up, fertilising the eggs internally. The female can produce more than 450 eggs, which she painstakingly lays one by one onto aquatic plant leaves in the water.

Not fussy in diet, they will eat anything small enough, with upland ponds often full of fly larvae and beetles to gorge on. Many of these ponds can dry out in the summer but this isn't an issue for the palmate newt, which can spend most of the summer on dry land.

BULLHEAD and STONE LOACH Cottus gobio and Barbatula barbatula

Fish life can be pretty sparse this high up in the catchment but the bullhead and stone loach do very well here. Both like good flows with clean water and plenty of rocks to hide under.

Bullheads (below left) have large, flat heads and usually grow to around 6cm, although they can reach twice this size. Voracious predators, they will eat most small invertebrates that cross their path, and even other small fish. They communicate with a series of grunts to attract a mate.

The stone loach (below right) is far more secretive, usually only coming out at night. It has a slender body with slimy skin, a tench-like tail with rounded edges and reaches a length of around 5cm. It has six barbels around the mouth, fleshy appendages used to taste the water for food. There is another species of loach called the spined loach, which is laterally compressed to help dig into the silt and sand of the riverbed and is more often found further downstream.

COMMON TOAD Bufo bufo

Common toads typically prefer larger ponds with some depth for them to spawn in. But unlike most amphibians they will also spawn in running water so you may see them around rivers, particularly around small sections near the source. While frogs create clumps of spawn, the toad has a string of spawn that it wraps around reeds and aquatic plants. The tadpoles hatch out soon after and are poisonous, keeping them relatively safe from predators. Toads are creatures of habit, returning to the same pond year after year. Sadly, this is leading to a decline in numbers due to ponds drying out and roads being built in the middle of their return routes.

The common toad is the largest toad in Europe. The females reach up to 15cm long, while males are often less than half this size. When it comes to mating, the male has to just hang on and hope for the best. Toads can create large balls when mating, with several males writhing and grabbing hold of each other to try to get to the female.

Most toads live for about 10 years, but some females have survived to more than 40 years of age. The eyes are a deep orange with horizontal pupils and the skin colour is usually a muddy brown or grey. As well as producing a toxin from glands in its head, the common toad will defend itself by inflating its body to look larger and making it a harder meal to catch and swallow. Its diet is mostly worms, beetles and slugs.

WATER SHREW Neomys fodiens

The water shrew is the largest species of shrew in Britain, reaching a body size of 9cm. If its size doesn't differentiate it from other British shrew species, it's also the only one with a bright white belly and dark back, likely used as counter-shading when swimming to help disguise it from possible predators.

To help with its aquatic life, its fur is much denser than that of other shrews and, even in the winter, this little mammal doesn't hibernate. Water shrews are competent swimmers, able to dive down to find prey such as freshwater shrimps. If they catch something larger, like a frog or a fish, they use a toxin in their saliva to help subdue their prey, and so effectively have a venomous bite.

Tricky to spot, they tend to hide away in thick undergrowth, only coming out to find food, but it's always worth checking the edges of small streams in case one is out.

Water shrews are fairly short-lived, around 19 months maximum, with breeding occurring throughout the summer. They produce two to three litters, each with 3–15 young, between April and September.

CURLEW Numenius arquata

Often thought of as a coastal bird, the curlew will also come inland to nest on moorland areas in the spring. Its bill is one of its signature features, with a long slender curve for picking out small worms and molluscs. The brown mottled colouration of its feathers helps it blend into long grasses when nesting.

Curlews have suffered huge declines in recent years, mainly thought to be due to changes in farming practices, an increase in predators such as corvids and foxes, and climate change. Between 1994 and 2010, there has been a 46 per cent decline in their numbers across England.

They prefer moorland, as the higher areas provide a dry nesting site, while the depressions and dips nearby have plenty of wet ground for long periods of the year where they can find their prey in the soil. Both male and female curlews are territorial, defending their nest site from rivals. They often return to the same nest site and keep the same partner year after year, which can be quite some time, with some birds living up to 30 years.

Their whistling 'cur-lee' call is one of the most familiar sounds across the moors during the summer and is the origin of their name.

GREY WAGTAIL *Motacilla cinerea*

Much more colourful than its name suggests, the grey wagtail has grey upperparts, a black and white tail and a bright yellow belly. The yellow wagtail, in comparison, is almost completely yellow, while the pied wagtail is a mix of whites, blacks and greys with no yellow. The grey also has a longer tail than the other two species. It is most often found by water, usually along the banks of small brooks, burns and babbles, where it looks for riverside insects to feed on. It often nests under bridges and steep banks by rivers where the fly life is plentiful in the summer, providing large amounts of food for the chicks.

It gets its name from its habit of bobbing its tail constantly, but the truth is that we don't know exactly why it does this. One theory is that it could be to help to flush out insects, but it's perhaps more likely that the tail movement has a social function, with individuals signalling to potential mates about the quality of their condition.

As they are dependent on water and insects for food, grey wagtails are particularly susceptible to cold winters, so can be seen moving south during cold blasts. The current breeding population in the UK is around 37,000 pairs, and they can be found on most rivers across the British Isles.

BUTTERBUR *Petasites hybridus*

This rhubarb-like plant can be seen carpeting the margins of upland rivers and fast-flowing streams. It is relatively widespread across most of Britain.

The name is thought to derive from people using its large heart-shaped leaves to wrap up butter during warm weather. Dense clusters of small, pale pink flowers emerge in early spring, on a bulbous stalk reaching up to 40cm high. The plant's stem and leaves are covered in lots of tiny hairs and have a felt-like texture.

Historically, butterbur has been used for many medicinal purposes, including reducing bleeding and relieving back pain and urinary problems and was even thought to help treat symptoms of the plague in the Middle Ages.

Mostly a marginal plant, it can be seen creating large rafts in the middle of rivers, offering shelter for many riverside species. After flowering, the plant dies down later in the year and regrows the following spring. It typically inhabits moist ground and spreads via its roots, creating rhizomes, so can cover large areas of the riverbank.

GOLDEN-RINGED DRAGONFLY Cordulegaster boltonii

This is the longest species of dragonfly in Britain or, specifically, the female is, as the ovipositor on the end of the tail makes her total length around 8.5cm. The male lacks this, and also has a club-shaped body rather than the straight-sided abdomen of the female.

The colours are striking on this dragonfly: black with bright yellow rings all around the body and (when fully mature) bright green eyes. It's the only dragonfly to have these kinds of markings in Britain so is easy to tell apart from other species.

Golden-ringed dragonflies prefer moving water to lay their eggs into, often around acidic bogs and moorland. These small slow-flowing streams are usually full of small invertebrates for them to prey on, and they are often the top predators in this microhabitat. The larvae are very well camouflaged, burying into the riverbed and waiting for prey to pass by. The larvae may be in the river for several years but the adults only have a short period on the wing, from May to September. Because they are large dragonflies, they can catch sizeable insect prey when adults, including damselflies, wasps, beetles and even other dragonflies.

CADDISFLY Trichoptera spp.

There are just under 200 species of caddisfly in Britain, and telling them apart can be tricky at best, with the young all having an aquatic phase. One of the characteristics that many share is the larva's habit of making a home out of debris from its watery environment. Some will use small stones, shells and even plant matter. This creates some shelter to hide away from potential predators.

As they aren't very quick-moving creatures, caddisfly larvae rely heavily on this makeshift shell. They use a kind of silk to stick the material together, though it varies between species (and some species don't have a shell at all). Some even create underwater nets like a spider's web to catch food being washed downstream.

The larvae move slowly on the riverbed to avoid detection but even this isn't enough to stop all predators, with dippers favouring them in particular. You can often tell a dipper hotspot by all the empty larval cases on a rock. The dipper shakes the grubs loose and leaves the shells behind.

When it is fully grown, the larva pupates and some weeks later the adult fly breaks free of the pupal case to find a mate. Adults are winged and slender-looking, like moths. They don't eat in the adult stage and are focused on finding a mate.

2

Upper Reaches

The part of the river known as the upper reaches is the point where it really starts to pick up its character and is more in line with what most people would think of when they picture 'a river'. You have white water crashing over rocks, with twists and turns in the shapes of the watercourse. It's often a damp and humid environment, with moss-covered rocks, fine mist in the air and banks covered with gnarly old trees. The river starts to become more of an obvious presence and influence in the environment, rather than just a little sliver of water. However, while wider than the source, the upper reaches are still an intimate place with the river often being narrow and jumpable in places. The bottom is littered with smooth clean pebbles and some sandy areas depending on the current. The clarity is generally pretty good, with some rivers as clear as gin, while others have a sepia peat hue to them if coming off moorland or heath.

← River Kennall, Kennall Vale Nature Reserve, Cornwall.

As a general rule of thumb, the upper reaches is also the part of the river that is least impacted by human activity in terms of chemicals and sewage, although this will depend on where you are in the country as the problems are worse in some areas than others. The lower you are down the river, the more chance pollutants, chemicals and other outside influences have had to leach in. As a result, the upper reaches can be a lifeline for many species, such as river flies, white-clawed crayfish and grayling that struggle with the barrage of problems that rivers face downstream.

Making yourself heard

As this part of the river is full of power, with water crashing against rocks, it's quite a noisy environment to live in, but many river creatures have found their own solutions to get round this. Species like dipper, kingfisher and otter all have high whistle-like vocalisations, which have a higher frequency than the babbling of the water, making them audible over the noise of the river. This means these animals are still able to communicate to find a mate and defend their territory. And it's not just the species above the water that have special techniques to cut through the clamour. The bullhead is a small bottom-dwelling fish that can, in effect, sing. In the spring, the male will grunt by rubbing the bones of his pectoral girdle against those of his skull. The aim of this low thudding serenade is to entice a female in to breed; as sound travels further in water, it's more likely to reach potential mates across the river.

One little insect that takes the acoustics to the extreme is the male lesser water boatman. What it lacks in size, being only about 1cm in length, it makes up for in noise, making the loudest noise of any animal relative to its body size. To make this colossal din, the male water boatman rubs his penis (or 'genitalia appendage') against the ridged surface of his abdomen, like a wooden spoon against a washboard. It's been recorded at up to 99.2 decibels, which is loud enough for people walking along the river to hear! All this is to attract a female boatman, who could be out of sight or hidden away, and entice her out to mate.

↓ Lesser water boatman.

→ When cows enter the river for a drink, they can cause major bank erosion.

Salmon saving the forests

In autumn, salmon move up into the upper reaches of rivers from the sea to spawn, bringing a mass influx of nutrients from the ocean deep inland. While some salmon will return to the sea (around 10 per cent of females are repeat spawners), the majority will die. Their bodies contribute an important part of the nutrient cycle, not just for the animals that live in and around upland rivers, but also for the surrounding trees. With the nutrients helping the trees to thrive, this in turn benefits species that rely on the trees for shelter and food, such as crested tit, pine marten and capercaillie, to name but a few. Healthy trees also help shade the river, keeping it cool, which the salmon prefer. And when the trees fall into the river, they create cover for salmon parr (juveniles), as well as shelter in floods. In a roundabout way, this creates a symbiosis between the salmon and the surrounding woodland, with both benefiting from each other's existence.

Cattle damage

As the upper reaches regularly run through farmland, the water is often accessible to livestock, which will go to the river to drink. This can cause a range of issues, particularly with cows, as they flatten the bankside vegetation and erode the riverbanks, sending a tsunami of mud directly into the river. This results in wider and shallower parts of the river that are full of mud and not much use to surrounding wildlife. The mud chokes the gravels, depriving fish of prime spawning habitat, and the murky water hinders photosynthesis for any aquatic plants that haven't already been eaten by the cows. The banks become more susceptible to flooding due to the cows mushing up all the soil, and excess nutrients are added to the river from the waste they produce going directly into the water. This excess waste causes huge algal blooms, which can make the water more turbid and carpet the riverbed in thick clumps of algae. This then prevents many aquatic plants from growing, as there's reduced sunlight and space on the riverbed. The algae also absorb more oxygen from the river, depleting a resource which is crucial for a whole host of fish, invertebrates and plants.

There is a fairly easy solution to this problem, which is to fence the river off and install a cattle trough to pump water up from the river, instead of allowing the cows down to the bank. This allows the vegetation on the banks to grow back, strengthening the bankside margins and stopping erosion. As well as creating healthier habitats for surrounding wildlife, it also means the farmer doesn't lose more land to soil erosion and less sediment enters the river.

Rebending rivers

Over millennia the inhabitants of Britain have been engineering rivers; from the Romans to the Victorians, we can't simply leave a river alone. The purpose is often to alter land for settlement and farming, draining wetlands and making travel easier by straightening and deepening rivers. This, however, diminishes habitat diversity, meaning fewer species are present. Straight rivers also cause more flooding by funnelling all the power in one direction; when the flow eventually does hit a corner, the banks can burst, causing them to erode.

Many groups are now working to 'rewiggle' rivers, putting the bends, meanders and corners back into the environment. It's a bit more manageable to do this in the upper reaches, where the river is smaller than further downstream. These twists and turns mean it takes longer for the water to get downstream and the curvature slows down the flow, adding storage capacity. This helps to reduce the risk of flooding. It also creates a more diverse habitat, with different depths, flows and substrate to suit a wider array of species and create a biodiversity hotspot. One prime example is the River Glaven in Norfolk at Bayfield. Prior to the work, the river

↓ River restoration on the River Glaven in North Norfolk to improve habitat for a myriad of species.

was a straight drainage ditch full of phosphates and silt, and with little flow. The Norfolk Rivers Trust in partnership with the Environment Agency and the Worldwide Fund for Nature (WWF) funded the work to put in a more diverse course, create ponds around the river and to import gravel for the riverbed. It's now home to many fish species like eel, lamprey and trout, and the biodiversity has increased.

If you were to leave a river to its own devices, it would rewiggle (or re-meander if you prefer) itself over time, but this could take decades and may impact the local area in negative ways (for example, if there's housing nearby). By digging a new course on the floodplain, we can simulate how the river should be. There has been a rise in river restoration, with over 2,500km restored in the UK since the early 1990s. However, this represents less than 3 per cent of the highly damaged river network, and much more needs to be done.

Birdwatching

In essence, all you need for birdwatching is a pair of binoculars and a willingness to stand by a bush for a couple of hours in the hope of seeing a small brown bird. But it can be much more complex than that. There are no hard and fast rules: if you want to find rarer birds across the country, there's scope for that but, equally, you could enjoy seeing what turns up in your local area. Rivers, of course, are a magnet for birds and the perfect place to spot species that are using them as a stop-off point on a migration route, as well as the more permanent residents that like the flowing water, such as dippers. I'll be honest, my favourite kind of birding is when I am walking along a riverside path and I get to see something so close that I can drop the binoculars and just take everything in. Birds living along many of the well-walked river paths are used to people, so you can often get a great view of them. If you're new to birdwatching, see the box below for some tips.

GETTING INTO BIRDWATCHING

- Many bird species can be quite shy, so **wearing dull colours is always a good idea.** You don't have to be dressed like you're in the SAS, but choosing to wear browns, black and greens is ideal.
- **Learning birdcalls is so useful to identify birds you can hear, but not see.** Going on guided bird walks will help with this, but there are also many sound-identifying apps, such as Merlin, that you can download for your phone.
- **There are many types of binoculars to choose from but I would recommend something along the lines of 8×42** (with 8 being the magnification and 42 referring to the diameter of the objective lens in millimetres), which is wide enough to search out birds and zoomed-in enough to actually work out what they are.
- When using binoculars, **keep looking at the bird and raise the binoculars to your eyes,** which should help you locate the bird and get a better look.
- **I like to keep notes of what I see either on my phone or in a little notepad.** If you can, submit what you see to local recorders, especially if it's a rarer bird.
- It can be nice to just wander off on your own, but birding can be a social event so why not **go with a friend, partner or local club to share the experience.**

Collecting seeds and stones

When you start to peer into the undergrowth and margins of the river it makes you appreciate all the components of this habitat, not just the more flashy aspects like kingfishers or waterfalls. These more subtle parts of the river are fantastic in their own right and having a small part of that to take home is a great reminder. It can also be a good way to encourage the kids to come along on a walk as there is a treasure-hunt sort of vibe when out looking for something specific.

I'm something of a magpie when it comes to collecting natural history items like bones, stones and seeds. Some seeds are easy to spot, like the large pods of yellow flag iris, which will be out at the end of the summer and full of large brown seeds; others are a bit harder to find, like ragged robin, which might be tucked away in the grassy margins of the river. The seeds can be collected (carefully and in moderation) to plant at home.

Unless the plant is protected it's legal to collect seeds, although the site itself may have restrictions if it's a Site of Special Scientific Interest (SSSI) or National Park, for example, so do check online if you're unsure. Don't take more than you need, and make sure you leave some to germinate in the area you are collecting from – and never take the whole plant. If you aren't sure what the plant is, check a field guide before handling it or take a photo and identify it at home. You don't want to handle a plant that could be poisonous, accidentally damage a protected species, or introduce something invasive to your garden which may be difficult to remove later.

As for stones, I'll be honest, I'm not a geologist but I can appreciate the colours and texture of granite, chalk and slate. When collecting stones, make sure you check the local laws in your area. On many beaches in Britain, for example, it's illegal to take stones as it can contribute to coastal erosion if too many are taken. Inland, there's no clear law on it but if you're unsure, it's probably best to seek the landowner's permission. I should say there's also absolutely nothing wrong with simply enjoying these things where they are!

One of my best finds was a millstone about the size of a dinner plate in the River Don in Sheffield: little bits of human history can also be uncovered when looking in the rivers.

TOP TIPS FOR COLLECTING

- **Collecting locally means the wildflowers are adapted to your climate** and so are more likely to thrive in your garden.
- **Some wildflowers need cold weather to germinate**, so be aware of this before you sow them.
- Why not **display your rocks and stones** in a small case that can be mounted on the wall to remind you of past trips?
- Similar to the Merlin app for birds, if you want to find out what rock you have, you can **download Rock Identifier: Stone ID** (or alternatively make friends with a geologist!).

→ Wild carrot seeds.

Where to visit

RIVER WYE, Chee Dale

If you've ever walked along the Monsal Trail, you'll be familiar with the wonderful Derbyshire Wye and its fast-paced watercourse. Derbyshire Wildlife Trust also manages an area of it at Chee Dale, which is a great site to see dippers, water voles and some of the country's only natural spawning rainbow trout. The trout were accidentally introduced in the 1800s from North America and have since slotted into the local ecosystem. The Derbyshire Wye holds an impressive amount of river fly species; boasting more than 200, it has more than any other river in Great Britain. While it's a great walk all year round, offering shade in the summer and some shelter from wind and rain in the winter, autumn is by far the best time to visit, with lots of fungi on show and extra water from rains making the river really rush down. It's also a little quieter than earlier in the year.

The Monsal Trail offers spectacular views of the river. The trail is 8.5 miles long, stretching between Blackwell Mill in Chee Dale and Coombs Road in Bakewell and close to Great Longstone, Little Longstone, Cressbrook Mill, Litton Mill and Tideswell Dale. It follows the old railway line of the former Manchester to London Midland Railway, which closed in the late 1960s. Be warned that it can get muddy and involves clambering over rocks at times, but from the stepping stones to its rocky gorges, it's a stunning walk.

At only 22 miles long, the river doesn't have many tributaries but the River Lathkill does join it before the Wye itself enters the Derwent. The Lathkill is a remarkable river, with incredibly clear water, with the famous writer Charles Cotton, describing it in *The Compleat Angler* (first published in 1653), as the 'purest and most transparent stream' he had ever seen. The river, thankfully, is still in relatively good health.

RIVER KENNALL, Cornwall

While most people think of Cornwall for its coastline, it's also home to a stunning little river called the Kennall. Cornwall Wildlife Trust manages part of an old gunpowder mining area, now the Kennall Vale Nature Reserve, which has been reclaimed by nature and is covered in various mosses, lichens and fungi thriving in this damp environment. It would have been part of the wider Atlantic rainforest that once covered the west of Britain, of which only a few pockets are left on the west coast.

With a licence granted in 1811 to manufacture explosives for the mining and quarry industries, the gunpowder works at Kennall Vale was one of the first of its kind in Cornwall. It is regarded as the best preserved gunpowder mine in the south-west. The gunpowder mill closed its doors in 1910 when advancements in blasting technology became more widespread and cheaper. It wasn't until 1985 that the Cornwall Wildlife Trust took over the reserve to manage it for the many woodland species that call it home.

The route around the Kennall Vale Nature Reserve is under two miles and circular, though can be steep at times. With dense woods and numerous abandoned buildings for roosting, the bat population is high here. They tend to roost in the old mines, so standing by any of them at dusk will offer a good chance of seeing several bat species, including brown long-eared bat, lesser horseshoe bat and greater horseshoe bat. The river itself often has grey wagtail and dipper along it and in the autumn sea trout can be seen spawning in its riffles. At 11 miles long, it's a relatively short watercourse, and apart from the Wildlife Trust reserve much of it is hard to access, but it's well worth a visit. You can park your car close to the reserve, but parking is limited. The Kennall joins the Carrick Roads estuary near Falmouth, where it flows into the River Fal.

RIVER NETHY, Cairngorms

Nethy Bridge is a popular destination for many birdwatchers visiting the Highlands due to its crested tits, capercaillies and crossbills, but the river from which it is named is also a special habitat. The name 'Nethy' is likely Gaelic in origin, meaning 'gleaming', which this small stream certainly is. The river rises in the Cairngorm Mountains, and unlike many Scottish rivers is quite clear, lacking the tea-stained colour of peat typical of most highland rivers. Running at around 16 miles in length, it is part of the Spey catchment, rising on the Saddle above Loch Avon before joining the Spey just downstream of Nethy Bridge. Abernethy Forest hugs the side of the river. 'Abernethy' means 'mouth of the River Nethy' and, as the name suggests, the Nethy meets the Spey close to the village.

In between the towns of Aviemore and Grantown-on-Spey, the river is a popular tourist route for rambling and camping. There are many walks that encompass the river range, from short trails to mountain hikes. The Castle Roy loop is around 3.5 miles long and takes you past the thirteenth-century castle of the same name, while the walk through Nethy Bridge itself has many bridges and paths along the river for good views of dippers, salmon and red squirrels.

Salmon move up into the Nethy in autumn from the Spey to spawn, and if you look for shallow gravelly patches, there's a good chance you will see this. Keep an eye out for depressions in the gravel; this will be the salmon's nest, called a redd. A decent frost will often trigger the spawning. If you're there in the summer, you may spot some of the many rare invertebrate species that the area is home to, such as the pine hoverfly, northern silver stiletto fly and northern damselfly.

A winter visit is also well worthwhile; with snow covering the banks and the river cutting through the environment like a knife, the landscape looks like something out of a fairytale.

RIVER COTHI, Carmarthenshire

The Towy is one of the largest rivers that flows entirely through Wales, and its largest tributary is the Cothi. In total the Cothi is 75 miles long, so not particularly long by any means, but what it lacks in length it makes up for in raw power and beauty. It rises up in the Cambrian Mountains, snaking its way past villages such as Abergorlech, Pumsaint and Pont-ar-Gothi. Hunched-over oaks and ash trees hug the Cothi's banks, and below the surface millennia of fast flows have carved out rocky crevices and caves in which the sea trout and salmon hide away in low summer flows. The name 'Cothi' comes from the Celtic for 'the place where the river sits', and so, like many UK rivers, is essentially a river named twice, i.e. 'River River'.

The woods along the Cothi are still home to some red squirrels, though numbers are dwindling due to squirrel pox brought in by invasive grey squirrels. The wet banks around the river offer good habitat for devil's-bit scabious, which in turn is the food plant for marsh fritillary butterflies, a species that is scarce in the rest of Wales. It is also noted for its sea trout fishing. Sea trout or 'sewin' as they are known in Welsh, are found all over Britain but Wales is perfect for them, with its many hills, valleys and mountains along with hundreds of rivers and streams, which run fast and cold. This is perfect for these game fish to spawn and thrive.

There's no path along the entire length of the river, as much of it passes through farmland, but there are routes that pass by it such as the Towy and Cothi Valley route, a 57-mile route that starts in Llandovery and takes you across hills, river valleys and farmland. Highlights along the way include Llandovery Castle, Paxton's Tower and Carreg Cennen Castle.

Species spotlight

WHITE-CLAWED CRAYFISH *Austropotamobius pallipes*

These are the largest native freshwater crustaceans in Britain and a good indicator of river health when present in decent numbers. Once widespread across the British Isles, the white-clawed crayfish is now confined to a fraction of its former range, mostly in isolated ponds and the upper reaches of rivers. The latter are often a last stronghold for them as the water is generally less polluted and it takes longer for the introduced signal crayfish (see page 102) to reach here, with fast flows and barriers slowing them down. As well as predating and outcompeting the white-clawed crayfish, the signal crayfish also carries a fungus poetically called the 'crayfish plague', which, while generally harmless to signal crayfish, is lethal to white-clawed crayfish. The two species can be surprisingly tricky to tell apart, as some white-clawed crayfish have an orange tint to their claws, which can be confused for the red 'signal' colour on a signal crayfish's claws. Signals, however, are typically much bigger, reaching up to 18cm long, while around 10cm is the maximum for white-claws. Signals also have a white calcium pocket on the intersection of their claws, which white-claws don't. It should be noted that white-clawed crayfish are protected and it is illegal to disturb them.

MANDARIN DUCK *Aix galericulata*

With perhaps a slight clue in the name, this is not a duck native to the British Isles. First brought over from China for waterfowl collections, it escaped in the twentieth century and they are now naturalised in much of Britain. Unlike many non-native species, mandarins appear to have little negative impact on native fauna and seem to have slotted in as a colourful extra. The males have dazzling colours and ornamentations in winter and spring, with orange plumes on their cheeks, orange 'sails' on their back and a violet breast. After breeding they are fairly drab, with a mix of browns and whites. As is fairly typical of ducks, the females are rather dull in comparison, with grey heads, brown backs and a white eyestripe. Unlike most ducks in Britain, they nest in cavities high up in trees. The population is thought to be around 4,400 breeding pairs in the UK, which is four times as many as those found in their native China. You'll often find them in groups or hanging around with mallards.

BROOK LAMPREY *Lampetra planeri*

The brook lamprey is the smallest of the three lamprey species found in Britain. These primordial fish have been around for more than 300 million years and are in fact so ancient that *we* are more closely related to a salmon than they are! Brook lampreys only grow to around 10cm long, and stay in the river their whole lives. Confusingly, there's also a species called a river lamprey, which looks very similar but it's around twice the size of the brook lamprey, at 20cm, and goes out to sea when adult. Unlike sea and river lampreys, which both feed on the blood of other fish, brook lampreys are filter feeders and spend most of their life hidden away in silt beds before emerging for a few days in the spring to spawn, making them quite tricky to spot. They like shallow clean riffles in the river to spawn, often with some cover nearby. The female creates a depression in the gravel called a redd, and multiple males will wriggle and writhe around her to encourage her to lay eggs.

Both males and females die shortly after spawning. If you are lucky enough to find them, these amazing creatures can be quite tame, and allow you to get really close to check them out.

BROWN TROUT *Salmo trutta*

A rather bland name for a fish that can come in such a variety of colour combinations, from buttery golds to fiery red spots. As well as the range of different colours, these fish come in many different sizes, from 6cm individuals that live in hill streams you can step across to 120cm monsters that go out to sea and feed on the rich pickings around our coast before returning to rivers to spawn. In fact, the brown trout comes in such a range of shapes and colours that it is the most genetically diverse vertebrate in the world. Large brown trout can be confused with salmon (see page 148), but on closer inspection the two are relatively easy to tell apart. The brown trout has a square or slightly convex tail, which is quite thick, while the salmon has a forked tail. The spots on a salmon typically stop below the lateral line (dots along the fish's flank used to sense movement in the water), while a trout will be more heavily covered all over the body. On the head, the salmon is more pointed with the mouth ending roughly in line with the eyes, whereas in the trout the mouth extends beyond the eye and the head is typically blunter. Native across the British Isles, brown trout are found in almost every healthy bit of water that can sustain them.

GRAYLING *Thymallus thymallus*

This salmonid has a touch of the tropical about it with its beautiful, distinctive dorsal fin. The fin is a mix of kingfisher blue, ruby red and deep purple – the kind of colour palette an artist would dream of. The male's fin is larger, used to attract a female. During courtship, he will erect it and flash it at other males in an attempt to intimidate them. If this fails, the male graylings will fight, bashing, head butting and slamming each other into submission. Once the other male is beaten, the victor will escort the female to some fine gravel where he drapes his dorsal fin over her and they spawn. Unlike salmon and trout, grayling aren't faithful to one particular site and will spawn in a larger, more sporadic area.

Grayling are generally a good sign of water quality: if the grayling are thriving, most other fish should too; if there's a water-quality incident, they are often the first to go.

The nose is pointed to help dig into the gravel for submerged prey but they will also rise to the surface to take insects. The scientific name *Thymallus* refers to the fish's smell, which has a hint of thyme about it.

WATER FORGET-ME-NOT *Myosotis scorpioides*

While many people will be familiar with terrestrial versions of this plant, there is also an aquatic species, which grows along the margins of riverbanks and ponds. They look very similar, but, along with their habitat preferences, another key difference is their lifespan, with the terrestrial species being biennial and the water forget-me-not being perennial.

It has small subtle flowers that bloom in June and are sky-blue (sometimes pink or white) with a yellow ring in the middle. Its scientific name comes from the curved 'tail' at the end of its stems, which also gives it its other common name of scorpion grass.

The plant can grow up to 45cm tall, but tends to sprawl out and can spread quickly using both seeds and rhizomes. It can be found rooted in the mud or as a floating plant weaving amongst other surface vegetation.

The origin of the name of this flower has an interesting tale. The legend goes that a knight was walking along a river with his lady when he saw the flowers and tried to pick them for her. However, he lost his balance and fell into the water, carrying the flowers with him. Before he drowned, he called out 'forget me not' to his lady. The lady named the flowers after him and wore them every day until she died.

DIPPER *Cinclus cinclus*

The classic upland stream bird, the dipper loves fast and clean water. Its call is a sharp whistle, which cuts through the noise of running water, a feature many riverine animals have developed (see also page 26). It earns its name well, bobbing up and down when moving along the river. It is thought that this dipping is a way of communicating visually with other dippers whilst living in a very loud environment. Interestingly, the British subspecies of dipper differs slightly from its European counterpart in that it's slightly more chestnut-coloured but still has the white throat.

    This is the only British songbird to live by the water all year round and, uniquely among songbirds, has dense rather than hollow bones, which helps it dive down into the water to find food. It uses its wings to fly underwater and catch invertebrates and small fish. Dippers can cope with quite fast flows, but during floods may retreat to ponds and side streams. An easy way to find dippers is to look for a rock that has lots of caddisfly remains around it, as a dipper will be using the rock to decant its prey from its shell. The other clue is the result of this food: a few white blobs of dipper poo!

STARWORT *Callitriche stagnalis*

Owing its name to its five leaves that form a classic star shape, starwort grows in large clumps that rise up to the surface and provide plenty of hiding places for many smaller species. It's sometimes called shrimp grass as it is often loaded with small *Gammarus* shrimps. Mainly found in still or stagnant water (hence the scientific name *stagnalis*) and the margins of slower-moving water, it's a great aquatic plant for invertebrates. It is favoured by newts to lay their eggs on as the leaves are the perfect size for the females to wrap their eggs around individually. Like many submerged plants, it's also an oxygenator, and helps to remove excess nutrients from the water. During the colder months it will die off, but seeds dispersed in the pond will germinate the following spring.

    The plant has a pale green colouration overall, with long stems poking out and teardrop-shaped leaves. It can flower in the summer but its minute white flowers are easy to miss. It has shallow roots that help attach it to the riverbed.

SNIPE *Gallinago gallinago*

These mottled brown, long-billed waders are often hidden in the undergrowth but can sometimes be seen on the water's edge, probing into the wet ground for small insects and worms. They use their cryptic colouration to blend into long grasses and reeds and can remain still to avoid predation. The upper reaches of rivers are often lined with these tufts of vegetation, providing ideal habitat for snipe, but the birds can be found throughout the river system. During the winter, we experience a huge influx of snipe from continental Europe with an estimated one million coming over to enjoy our milder and wetter winters. The influx starts in October and most leave in the spring, although there is also a small resident population.

Male snipe produce an eerie and alien sound known as 'drumming'. As it flies downwards, the male sticks out its two outer tail feathers at a near 90-degree angle to its body, and when it reaches speeds of 30–53mph the feathers start to vibrate in the wind. The faster the bird dives through the air, the higher the pitch of the sound created. Male snipe do this as a way of attracting a mate and demonstrating their fitness. There is another species called the jack snipe, which is smaller in size, has a shorter bill and the top of its head is completely dark, lacking the smart golden central stripe that the common snipe has.

SCARLET ELF CUP *Sarcoscypha coccinea*

Few large fungi live underwater, but many microscopic fungi species play vital roles in river ecology both under the water and along its margins. The banks and margins of rivers, however, play host to many larger and vibrant species such as the scarlet elf cup (or elf cap). Its common name derives from its cup-like shape; in folklore, it is said that wood elves would drink from the cups. Below the cup is a short white stalk, which has a leathery feel to it.

With the upper reaches of many rivers being wooded, they provide a damp, dark environment perfect for the elf cup. Elf cups grow on rotting trees, especially maple and lime, with the fungus being most visible over the autumn and winter. The fungi can be found in clumps along dead branches, often surrounded by moss – the light green of the moss really showcases the vivid red cup against it. It can also grow in bundles on the ground. One of the unusual things about this fungus is that it makes a slight puffing sound when it releases spores into the air. While it's not a poisonous mushroom, it's not considered edible and is best avoided for the table.

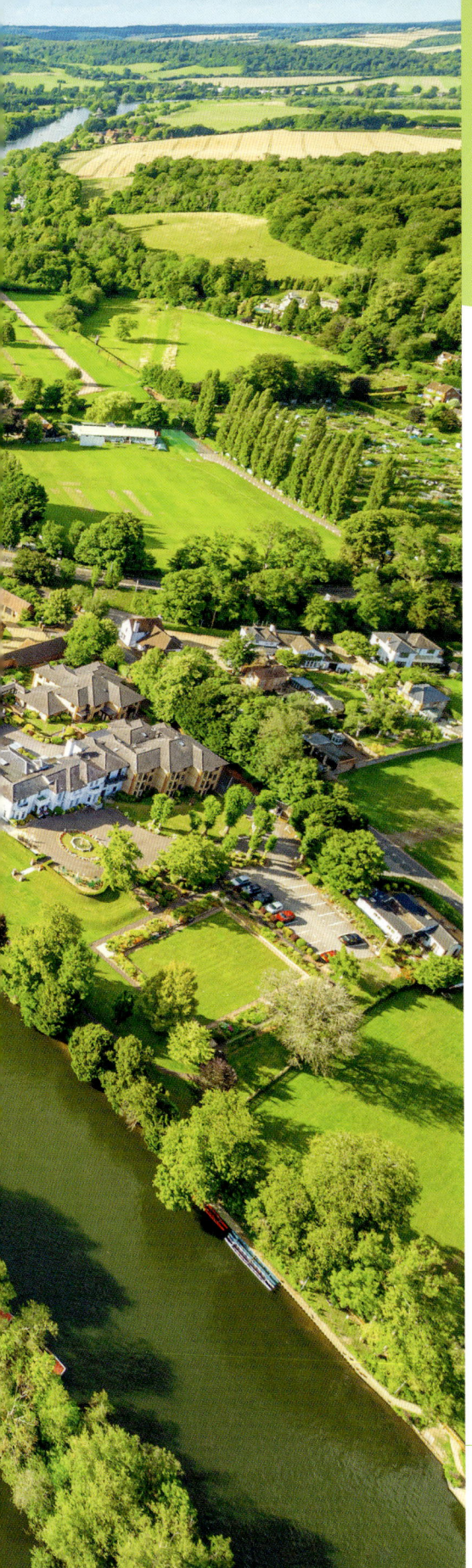

3

Middle Reaches

The middle reaches are often overlooked by many people, not having the charm and cleanliness of the upper reaches yet lacking the scale and diversity of the lower reaches. However, they are an important gateway between these two worlds and hold a fantastic mix of species.

Here, the river starts to widen out, and while there is still flow, this will often ease up in places, which allows for a greater mix of species that would shun the faster water upstream. There's also more room for plants to grow and, in places, great beds of ranunculus, yellow waterlily and willow moss can carpet the riverbed if the clarity and water quality is sufficient.

The riverbed is less polished here, with thin layers of mud and algae in the slower parts of the river. On the surface, you will often see subtle swirls giving a clue that a large rock or other object is below the surface, pushing up the water to reveal its location.

← River Thames, Henley-on-Thames, Oxfordshire.

Returning lost species

Rewilding is a broad term meaning different things to different people but, in essence, is a case of restoring a natural landscape that has been degraded by people, and this can include the reintroduction of lost species to rivers.

The truth is that we have lost many species in Great Britain, and more often than not it's because of humans: so is it not our moral duty to try to bring some back if possible? Our rivers have had their share of species come and go, with beavers, for example, being present until around 400 years ago when they became extinct in mainland Britain due to hunting for their thick fur, meat and castoreum, which comes from the beaver's anal glands and was traditionally used in perfume and food additives. Despite having not been around for the last four centuries, their presence is still felt in areas like Beverley, East Yorkshire, which was named after its beavers, and in the form of legacy ponds created by beavers, which still persist today. Beavers are also now being released back into former strongholds (see also pages 53 and 143).

In more recent years, the burbot (see also page 68), a freshwater cod, had its last confirmed sighting in 1969 before being declared extinct in England. Although a few romantics hold out hope that a burbot or two could still be swimming around, I'm afraid it's just not possible. A female burbot can produce up to 1 million eggs and if these fish were still here, someone would have come across them in the last 50 years. The Norfolk Rivers Trust is working to source fish from Belgium, the closest relatives to our own burbot, and in time return the species to some of its old haunts in Norfolk.

The majority of these lost species provided vital roles to the ecosystem, and their absence has left the British landscape as a jigsaw puzzle with some of its pieces missing. Many species just can't recolonise on their own, and if they are to make a return to their historic range, some human intervention is required.

Barriers on rivers

In Britain, humans have been altering the natural course and features of the rivers for hundreds of years, which has meant 97 per cent of rivers are fragmented by barriers like weirs. This intensified after the First World War, with 36 per cent of the river network of England and Wales, some 22,000 miles, now subject to major modifications. An even larger area is routinely maintained through practices such as the annual removal of silt or vegetation. This has all culminated into rivers being restrained and reshaped out of all natural recognition.

The main reason weirs are put into rivers is to control the flow, which can help with navigation or flood prevention, but other barriers include sewage pipes, sluices and turbines. These riverside barriers can create a multitude of problems for river wildlife. The most evident one is that they prevent fish moving upstream on migration.

← The moor frog was once found across Britain and is a prime candidate for reintroduction.

Salmon are perhaps the most famous example of this, but many species have become much rarer because they are totally cut off by barriers upstream, including European sturgeon, smelt, shad and lamprey.

Unlike salmon, these other species can't jump very well, so even relatively small barriers stop them in their tracks, and in a matter of years they die out in river courses. All of these fish would have been far more widespread before river barriers. It's important to note that even if fish can jump over a barrier, they expend a huge amount of energy in doing so, which means they have less energy left for spawning. Fish are also far more susceptible to predation while they are being held back behind a weir. Salmon smolts (juveniles transitioning from freshwater to saltwater environments), for example, are targeted relentlessly by pike, seals and fish-eating birds at human-made barriers on their return to sea. The barriers also create huge banks of silt above them that trap chemicals and heavy metals, retaining them in the river. As well as polluting the water, this also means that many fish that want to spawn on gravel can't do so above the weir where the gravel should be cleaner, because the riverbed is buried beneath a layer of silt.

↑ Chester Weir has a fish pass and salmon counter on it to allow easy monitoring of the river's fish.

→ Otter spraint (droppings) by the River Thet, Thetford.

Finding poo!

You might think there's enough poo floating around our rivers currently, but looking on the banks of rivers for animal droppings can be a great way of finding out what's living in the area, even if you don't spot the animals themselves. Birds generally leave behind white liquid poos because they excrete the nitrogenous waste as uric acid, which forms a white, sticky paste. So, for example, if you see lots of white paste on a rock in the river, there's a good chance it's a favourite hangout of a dipper. Or, if you look a bit higher up the banks into bushes and overhanging

MIDDLE REACHES

→ Viewing window at the Diglis Fish Pass, River Severn.

branches, you might see streaks of white poo, which is a good sign of a kingfisher perch. They will often return to the same productive feeding spots, so it's worth looking out for them.

Mammal poo can be a bit easier to find, with otter droppings or 'spraint' being the classic poop-finder's prize. The poos are around 1–3cm long. Otters tend to poo on hard surfaces as the smell of the spraint will last longer. This is a key means of communication, giving other otters information about whose territory they're in, the health of the individual that left the spraint, and if a female is in heat (when poo becomes a bit like messages on an otter version of a dating app). It's said that the spraint smells of jasmine, though I've always found it to just be fishy!

American mink faeces, on the other hand, absolutely stink. The scat normally contains more fur, feathers and bones than an otter spraint due to minks' more varied diet. Mink scats tend to be long and tapered, while otter spraints are more coarse and messy.

Water voles tend to have a latrine and the poos are about the size and shape of a Tic Tac sweet. These latrines are normally near the burrows and the faeces have a green colour to them.

Windows into rivers

If you're interested in seeing what's going on within a river, without the risk of getting wet, the viewing window on the River Severn at Worcester offers a unique opportunity to do so. Completed in 2021, the Diglis Fish Pass allows more than 27 species of fish to move upstream freely, with rare species like twaite shad, salmon and sea lamprey being seen. You can book a slot at the viewing window from March to October to get a glimpse of the species that call the Severn home. The underwater viewing gallery allows you to see the various fish and, if you're lucky, even otters. Every few weeks the Canal & River Trust, who maintains the pass, cleans the window and checks the structure of the pass. I highly recommend going to visit it and I think every major river in the UK should have one!

Further north, the first viewing window to be opened was at Pitlochry Dam, connecting the River Tummel to Loch Faskally. The fish ladder below is 310m long, with pools helping salmon leapfrog up and a viewing window allowed visitors to see salmon moving up. Unfortunately, in 2019 it was shut for health-and-safety reasons, but a live webcam is available in the visitors centre.

Fishing

Fishing is perhaps the only riverside hobby where you might sit in a single area for the entire day, giving the angler a unique opportunity to take in all the minute details of a river environment: the

TIPS FOR BEGINNERS

- **Look into joining a local fishing club** so that you can benefit from the support of more experienced anglers.
- Fish welfare is paramount! Make sure to **wet your hands before holding any fish and return fish to the water** as quickly as possible.
- Different parts of the river will hold different species, so **learn about the habits of fish to get a better idea of what you're likely to catch** in your chosen area. For example, barbel like faster water, while bream prefer it slower.
- I try to **travel light, carrying just what I need** so I can explore different sections of the river. However, staying in the same spot can reap its own rewards in certain locations and can be a good option if you're less mobile.
- **It's not all about size!** Smaller species like gudgeon, ruffe and dace often have wonderful markings and can be more of a challenge to catch.
- As with any outdoor pastime, **take any litter home with you**. Angling line can also be recycled.

willow trees swaying, the flow of the water and the birds singing. I've often been sat on the bank and had long-tailed tits or a wren come in close (of course I never have my camera with me!).

Because of their intense concentration on the water, anglers are often the first to notice when something isn't right in the river, for example spotting sewage fungus along the bottom or dead fish at the side.

To fish in England or Wales on fresh water, you need a rod licence from the Environment Agency (you don't need one to fish in Scotland). This doesn't mean, however, that everywhere is free, and you may need to pay the landowner to fish.

All rivers in England and Wales are closed to coarse fishing (fishing for freshwater species other than salmon or trout) from 15 March to 15 June to allow fish to spawn in peace. In Scotland there is no salmon fishing allowed by law on Sundays. Make sure you familiarise yourself with the local by-laws in the area where you intend to fish, as rules can vary across regions.

↓ Fly-fishing in the evening.

Paddling

Exploring waterways on a paddle board, canoe or kayak can be a fantastic way to immerse yourself in the riverine environment, as being on the water level allows you to experience the river from a completely different perspective. You can also cover miles of water, seeing each bend, riffle and pool as you pass by. It's important to note that you need a waterways licence to paddle on most canals and rivers in England and Wales. This is easily obtained online, but doesn't cover all rivers so it's best to check beforehand. In Scotland it's much simpler and, like most of mainland Europe, you can pretty much paddle wherever you like. Before you try a river for the first time I would suggest trying a lake or canal to get used to the basics and go out with a group to learn how to paddle safely.

GETTING STARTED WITH PADDLING

- This may sound obvious, but **make sure you have a life jacket on,** especially if paddling in faster water.
- When kayaking, **keep your centre of balance by sitting in the middle** of the kayak and **hold the paddle the same distance from each end.** Canoes and sit-on kayaks are more stable, so may be better for beginners than a sit-in kayak, but are heavier and less agile.
- **Keep an eye on weather and tides.** If the river is very high, it's safer to wait a few days for it to subside. Strong currents and high river levels can potentially be life-threatening.
- **Check access rights,** as it can be unclear as to whether or not you can launch or land in certain areas. Even if you can pass through some water, it may be considered trespassing if you come to shore on private land.
- If you are feeling particularly helpful, why not **collect litter** that has washed into areas other water users can't get at, helping to remove plastic from the river?

↓ Kayakers enjoying the River Stour.

MIDDLE REACHES

Where to visit

RIVER RIBBLE, Ribchester

This 75-mile-long river begins as a gentle flow of water 246m above sea level at Gayle Beck, close to Ribblehead Viaduct in the Yorkshire Dales National Park.

The Ribble crosses into Lancashire, where it slows down and becomes more like the middle reaches of a river, passing through lots of agricultural land. On the final stretch of its journey, it navigates Preston and meets the Irish Sea at the Ribble Estuary, near Lytham. It has several tributaries including the Calder, Hodder, Darwen and Douglas. The Hodder has a steep descent, starting at 400m above sea level and dropping to 99m in less than nine miles, and has some fast and impressive-looking falls.

The name 'ribble' comes from the Brittonic meaning 'great upland stream'. The Ribble actually has one of the largest tides in England. Spring tides can see tides run in at 5mph, causing a bore that runs inland like a mini tidal wave up to 11 miles upstream.

Over the years, the river has been heavily modified. This included work to divert it from its natural course to allow the development of Preston Dock, with the straight channel carrying the river out to the estuary. In 1840, the river was trained by the construction of a low rubble wall, straightening and deepening the course to allow navigation to the docks. The surrounding marshes and salt marsh areas have been extensively drained and fertilised, with much of the marshland converted to agricultural land by the mid-sixteenth century.

There is a riverside walk called the Ribble Way, which stretches for 65 miles, going through the towns of Preston, Ribchester, Rathmell and Ingleborough to mention a few. The route passes through a variety of landscapes including tidal marsh, open moorland and limestone gorges, linking the Lancashire Coast to the Yorkshire Dales National Park. For some bizarre reason there is a high number of hybrid fish of the chub x roach variety on the river at Ribchester, likely due to their spawning habitats being close by. On other rivers, these hybrids are very rare.

RIVER WENSUM, Norwich

The Wensum is the largest chalk-fed river in Norfolk and a tributary of the Yare, which it joins at Whitlingham. It starts near Colkirk, 80m above sea level, and has a few tributaries of its own, including the Tat, Tud and Ainse.

The Wensum aptly takes its name from the Anglo-Saxon word for 'winding'. This slower watercourse on the fringes of Norwich has many bars, pubs and even the Norwich City football ground along its banks, with one of the ground's stands formerly known as the River Stand. The river also passes the city's 900-year-old cathedral. Norfolk is synonymous with water mills, and the Wensum has 14, some dating back as far as the fifteenth century, such as Bintry Watermill near the village of Bintree. Most were not used to mill flour, as you might expect, but were instead used to drain the land.

The Wensum is a fantastic river to spot otters, and these normally shy animals can sometimes be seen in broad daylight in the middle of town. The river has a pathway called the Wensum Way, just over 12 miles in length, which passes through some beautiful central Norfolk landscape, much of it alongside or close to the river. It links the Nar Valley Way at Gressenhall with the Marriott's Way at Lenwade, passing through rural landscape between Gressenhall and Swanton Morley, then following the river valley, abundant with wildlife, through to Lenwade. It's a flat and gentle walk throughout its length. Most of the lowland chalk streams in Britain are found in Norfolk, and as it's the flattest and driest county in England, the rivers face various human-made pressures, especially from agricultural run-off.

RIVER AVON, Bath

The Avon runs for 83 miles, starting in the Cotswolds at 18m above sea level and ending in the Severn Estuary. In Bath, the river starts to slow, and is a centrepiece of the historic city. It is also where the Kennet and Avon Canal joins the river, and downstream the river itself becomes navigable.

With the Avon going into both Bristol and Bath, there are plenty of good riverside paths, including the 23-mile-long River Avon Trail, which starts in Pill and ends in Pulteney Bridge. It's a nice level walk, with great views of the Avon Gorge, Bristol Harbour and Bath. The Avon Gorge is a spectacular site and well worth a visit for a short walk, the path here being only 1.5 miles long. It sits to the west of Bristol city centre and is carved from limestone rock. It is rich in fossils dating back 350 million years, and is home to many specialist species such as peregrine, Bristol rock cress, Bristol onion and lesser horseshoe bat.

Species such as grey wagtail and kingfisher can be spotted right in the middle of Bath and beavers are now found on much of the Avon. Being close to many populated areas, access is generally pretty good, with many people enjoying kayaking, fishing and birdwatching along its banks. There are also many riverside cafés, pubs and shops so you can enjoy the river and its wildlife, alongside access to more urban facilities.

The name 'Avon' is from the Common Brittonic *abona*, 'river', which survives in the Welsh word *afon*. There are several other River Avons across Britain, so this one is often referred to as the Bristol Avon. The Avon meets a number of tributaries including the River Marden, Somerset Frome and River Chew, and smaller streams such as the By Brook, Brinkworth Brook and the River Trym. Along with Bath and Bristol, the Bristol Avon goes through other many towns including Malmesbury, Chippenham, Melksham, Bradford-on-Avon and Keynsham.

RIVER WYE, Hereford

The Wye is the fifth longest river in Great Britain at 155 miles long, starting in the Welsh mountains at Plynlimon, 600m above sea level and joining the Severn at Chepstow. The river in its lower reaches forms part of the Welsh and English border. The middle reaches of this river, however, stretch from around Hereford to Ross-on-Wye, where it's popular for kayaking and fishing for species such as barbel. The barbel isn't actually native to the Wye but was introduced for angling in the 1950s.

In recent years, the river has had a sharp decline in water quality, largely due to exponential growth in the number of intensive poultry units up and down the river valley. As of July 2020, in the counties of Shropshire, Herefordshire and Powys there are 500 farms with a total of 1,420 intensive poultry units, containing more than 44 million birds. The run-off of nutrients from chicken excrement from these farms is believed to have led to a major increase of phosphate levels in the river catchment in the past six years, causing the river to now exceed permitted levels of phosphates under the European Union (EU) Habitats Directive.

When its waters aren't running green, this is one of the most stunning rivers in Britain. It used to be full of flowing water-crowfoot and was one of the best salmon rivers in Wales. It's still pretty, but a shadow of its former self.

The Wye Valley walk is 136 miles long, starting at Rhyd-y-benwch car park, Hafren Forest in Mid Wales and ending at Chepstow Castle. The route is broken up into different sections for shorter, more manageable walks. It is fairly accessible all year but certain stretches can be quite muddy and wet in the winter, though a frosty walk in the river valley can be well worth it. The walk takes you right through Hereford so there's plenty of town parking if you want to explore this part of the river.

Species spotlight

OTTER *Lutra lutra*

There are very few success stories with modern wildlife in the UK, but the otter is one of them. In the late 1950s, otters were threatened with extinction due to the use of the chemical DDT in agriculture, which made its way into the food chain and reduced their breeding success. The chemical was eventually banned in the 1990s, allowing otter populations to recover. Some areas of the country never lost otters, such as the south-west of England, west Wales and northern England, and so they were able to spread out from these strongholds and recolonise old haunts. They are now starting to be found all over Britain again. There have also been some deliberate reintroductions in areas such as Norfolk.

Otters are top predators, taking fish, crayfish and birds. Mostly nocturnal, they can sometimes be seen in the day, especially those living on the Scottish coast, which hunt according to the tides rather than specifically coming out at night.

A male otter, called a dog otter, will have a large territory of up to 20 miles, which may encompass a few females in that range. Unusually for most British mammals, otters don't have a specific breeding season and will mate as soon as a female comes into heat. The female has a litter of up to four cubs, which she'll look after for up to a year.

BLACK POPLAR *Populus nigra*

Regarded as Britain's most threatened native timber tree, the black poplar is a species in trouble. Often found in boggy and wet areas, river valleys are its favoured habitat. It's estimated that only 7,000 trees are spread across Britain, with just 600 of these being female, making pollination very difficult. One of the other problems they face is hybridisation with other poplars – because there are more female trees of other species, the black poplars pollinate with these instead and so create more hybrids than true black poplars.

These trees have a rounded shape, with fairly thin branches. The leaves are a rich green colour, and in spring the male poplars produce red catkins with a sweet scent to them. The bark is greyish-brown, which can go black over time.

Black poplars were once popular for building wooden-framed houses as their wood is less flammable than most timbers, and its shock-resistant properties meant it was also used to make carts and floorboards, as well as various other items.

Black poplar was also a favourite tree to plant in cities, as it prefers heavy soil and damp conditions and is surprisingly tolerant of pollution.

PIKE *Esox lucius*

The top underwater predator of British waterways, the pike has a slender body from which it derives its name, resembling a medieval spear. Younger individuals have a stripy pattern to help them

blend in and hide from cannibalistic adults. As they mature, these markings become more blotched and the colours deepen to green and cream.

The mouth is lined with rows of razor-sharp teeth designed to grip slippery prey. Pike mostly feed on other fish, taking surprisingly large prey, which they will digest head first and slowly swallow the rest of the fish when it can fit! They will also feed on water voles, frogs and even birds up to the size of a coot. They are ambush predators, hiding away in weeds and moving at incredible bursts of speed to engulf prey with their large mouths.

Females grow several times larger than males, with the British record exceeding 21kg. They spawn in late winter, with several males cautiously chasing down a female until she releases thousands of eggs into submerged vegetation.

BARBEL *Barbus barbus*

The barbel is the king of the middle reaches, perfectly designed for life in flowing water. It has strong muscles in the tail to help it push up in strong flows and a sloped head to enable it to keep towards the riverbed when feeding.

When young, the barbel can be confused with the gudgeon. The quickest way to tell the two species apart is by the number of fleshy whiskers (also called barbels) around their mouths: barbel have four whiskers whilst gudgeon only have two. Young barbel are speckled, to help them blend in with their surroundings, but as they grow, they become a deep bronze and the fins take on a pink hue.

This species can grow to more than 9kg, and is one of the most popular coarse fish that anglers target on rivers, with some fishing spots on the River Trent, for example, being booked up years in advance. Barbel are only native to rivers that flow eastwards but over the years, mostly for angling purposes, have been introduced to rivers such as the Severn, Hampshire Avon and the Clyde.

They spawn in the summer, requiring warm water to trigger the process, with the males jostling for prime position to spawn in clean gravels with a much larger female.

EUROPEAN BEAVER *Castor fiber*

Beavers are the largest European rodents, with dense brown fur and a distinctive paddle-like tail. In 2009, beavers were legally reintroduced to Scotland, although it's worth noting that beavers have been on the Tay catchment since at least 2001. Since then, beavers have been encouraged to recolonise in large enclosures and some wild populations have popped up across England, including the River Otter in Devon.

Beavers are herbivores, so don't eat fish and mostly stick to vegetation within 20m of the riverbank. Their dams and beaver ponds are biodiversity hotspots, giving homes to many invertebrates, amphibians and plants. Although some migratory fish can be hindered by beavers on smaller rivers, there are benefits for them also, with the dams and ponds providing a safe nursery for young fish, and a feeding ground.

WATER SCORPION *Nepa cinerea*

With a rather misleading name, this is not actually a scorpion but an insect. Its long tail is used a bit like a snorkel, positioned near the surface to extract oxygen, and does not sting. Its claws, however, are less harmless and are used to grapple with prey, from tadpoles to other aquatic invertebrates. The water scorpion will then pierce the victim with its sharp proboscis, drinking its insides.

It is not especially big, with individuals rarely reaching 4cm. The species prefers slack water with plenty of vegetation to hide away in.

It will sometimes leave water to find a new home and can fly but will more often crawl. To attract females, the male can make a chirping noise by rubbing its legs together a bit like a cricket. The female will then lay eggs onto aquatic plants, which hatch out after a month or so.

Water scorpions are sometimes known as 'toe biters', and larger species outside the UK have been known to pierce people walking barefoot. However, there is no record of this happening with the species we have here in Britain.

MIDDLE REACHES

GIANT HOGWEED *Heracleum mantegazzianum*

Native to Central Asia, giant hogweed is an invasive plant that somewhat resembles a large cow parsley, to which it is related. This riverside menace blocks out the light for native plants and can dominate the water's edge. Its seeds often fall into the water and are carried downstream, spreading elsewhere. Like many invasive plants, it started off as an ornamental addition to gardens in the early nineteenth century before escaping into the wild.

The 'giant' part of its name is no exaggeration. It can grow up to 5m tall and spread out to 2m – this is a beast of a plant. The leaves are reminiscent of rhubarb, with spiky hairs on the stem. The flowers, which are produced around June or July, are small and white, growing in large umbrella-like clusters.

It is perhaps best known for its unpleasant defence mechanism. The sap of giant hogweed contains a chemical called furocoumarin, which makes skin extremely sensitive to sunlight. Therefore, when people try to cut this plant down and get covered in its sap, it causes very painful burns and sores when the affected skin is exposed to sunlight. This can continue for months after contact. If you are unlucky enough to get some sap on you, it is best to wash as much off as possible and seek medical attention if needed.

PURPLE LOOSESTRIFE *Lythrum salicaria*

Purple loosestrife is a staple of the middle reaches of rivers, and in late August and September its covering of bright purple flowers offers a fantastic source of nectar for the last of the summer's insects to stock up on.

The stems are tall and slender, with thin light green leaves and flowers that grow in long spikes and gradually bloom from the bottom to the top. A perennial, it often dies off in the winter to come back the following summer. It prefers areas with poorly drained soil, making riverbank margins ideal, but it can be found growing in the water as well. A lover of full sun, it can form dense patches along the river.

It has associations with a number of insects, from the black-margined loosestrife beetle, which feeds predominantly on the leaves, to the loosestrife root weevil, whose larvae feed on roots and the adults gorge on the leaves.

Purple loosestrife spreads in two ways: by seeds falling off the dead stems in late summer, which can be washed downstream and germinate in wet soil, and by the roots spreading out and growing new shoots.

EUROPEAN BITTERLING *Rhodeus amarus*

This small, unassuming member of the cyprinid family has perhaps the most bizarre and intriguing way of spawning of any freshwater fish in Britain. Around May, the female bitterling extends a long tube called an ovipositor to lay her eggs inside a living freshwater mussel. The male, in a most brilliant collection of reds, blues and blacks, then fertilises the eggs. Although the eggs are inserted directly into the mussel, this doesn't seem to do the mussel any harm. The eggs will stay there, protected for a few weeks, before hatching out.

Males are quite territorial and will chase away rivals. When a female shows some interest in a male, he'll wiggle around her and, if she likes his dance moves, will lay the eggs.

Bitterling look a bit like a small bream with a deep body, but they only grow to the size of a 50p coin. These little fish aren't actually native to Britain but were introduced to England, probably via the aquarium trade. They cause little issues with native fish, however, and seem to slot into the environment with minimal disturbance. They like the slower reaches and weedy water, where they hang around in shoals. They have a patchy distribution, and are mostly found in Cheshire, Norfolk and Cambridgeshire.

GREY HERON *Ardea cinerea*

One of the most common waterbirds in Britain, grey herons are found throughout the river system. Typically solitary, they do buck this trend in early spring when they nest in trees communally, sometimes with other heron species such as little egrets.

Grey herons are among the earliest-nesting birds in Britain, sometimes starting in January. This is to take advantage of the glut of amphibians and early spawning fish at the beginning of spring.

Although grey makes up a good proportion of the bird's plumage, adults have a black crest on the head. The bill is usually yellow but those of males will have a hint of purple in the breeding season.

When hunting prey by the margins, the grey heron can remain completely still, waiting for any sign of prey, and strike with incredible speed to impale its next meal. To help spot prey, it has huge yellow eyes that allow it to use binocular vision to judge distance. It can also direct its eyes downwards to scan an area below the bill while keeping its head still, which helps it to avoid detection by fish.

4

Lower Reaches

In the lower reaches, a river will start to widen and spill out onto low ground, creating wetlands and a patchwork of ponds, lakes and ditches. This part of the river can be deceiving, as the surface often appears still but the flows beneath can be fast. The edges of the river and wetlands are festooned with reeds, grasses and clumps of other marginal plants. The bottom of the river here is covered with debris and detritus from rotting plants, wood and other items washed downstream.

With this huge concentration of water, and water plants such as reeds, these areas are hugely important carbon traps. Not only do the plants absorb carbon but also the mud beneath buries and traps it underground. 'Blue carbon', as it's known, absorbs 50 per cent of the carbon emitted into the atmosphere. With global temperatures continuing to rise, these habitats are vital to help fight climate change.

← RSPB Leighton Moss, Lancashire.

Agricultural pollution

While sewage in our rivers has gained a lot of public and media attention in recent years – and rightly so – there is another, arguably much worse cause of pollution: agriculture.

In essence, agricultural pollution is when chemicals from farmland enter the river. This could be excess nutrients from slurry or fertiliser spread on the fields, or more toxic concoctions such as pesticides.

Eighty-three per cent of English rivers have evidence of high pollution from sewage and agriculture, with no single stretch of river in England in good overall health. According to the 2024 State of Rivers report, toxic chemicals persist in every stretch of English rivers. Inevitably, this affects all of the plants and animals that live in and around the river.

Huge amounts of silt and soil also get washed off these cultivated fields when they are compacted or left without a cover crop. Heavy rain, especially in the winter, washes the mud into drains and sometimes directly into rivers, carrying all the nasty chemicals with it. As well as infecting the river with pollutants, it carpets the riverbed with mud that chokes the gravels. This means species that would normally hide in the gaps between the gravel, such as caddisfly larvae and bullheads, can no longer do so. It also reduces suitable habitat for fish that like to spawn over gravel, such as trout, chub and barbel.

Riverside buffers

One of the ways to at least slow down agricultural run-off is by allowing riverside buffers to grow. These strips of marginal vegetation act as a physical barrier that slows down pollutants entering the river and absorbs the nutrients. They also provide a rougher surface, which helps to catch mud and prevents it from getting washed away. That mud can then be used for future crops.

The buffers can be anywhere from 4m to 12m wide, depending on the space available and the kind of crop being farmed. It's not a permanent solution, but it does have the added bonus of creating miles of fantastic habitat for wildflowers and pollinating insects, which in turn pollinate crops. It also creates a highway for larger creatures, such as otters, foxes and badgers, to move along the riverbanks in relative safety and find new territories.

Of course, these buffers take up valuable

↓ Pesticides and fertilisers can sometimes leach from the fields into the rivers.

↑ Silver-washed fritillary. Riverside buffers of vegetation alongside fields can provide vital habitat for pollinators.

farming land, and so many farmers will need government subsidies to be able to allow space for them.

A safe place to stop

As the lower reaches of a river are larger and interconnected with wetlands, they offer a range of habitats from thick reedbeds to boggy woodland and shallow muddy banks. This makes them biodiversity hotspots, supporting a mixture of specialist species that like both still and running water.

They are also an important stop-off for migrating birds – think of them like a motorway service station. Birds can rest up and feed, making the lower reaches a great place to find migrant birds in the spring and autumn, allowing people to see many different species in a condensed area. These open areas are great for both birdwatching and photography.

Keeping dry and warm

For many bird and mammal species that live in rivers, there are two things that are crucial: keeping dry and keeping warm. Birds that spend a lot of time in the water, such as goosanders, use the tight mesh of their feathers as a shell to trap air between the skin and the feathers, creating a buffering layer that protects the skin from water and keeps the cold out. They also have preen oil, which comes from a gland above the tail. While on dry land, birds will regularly rub the oil onto their bill and then onto their feathers. This improves the feathers' condition and can make them better able to resist moisture.

Cormorants do not trap air against their skin. Instead, their feathers compress tightly to the body and reduce their buoyancy, meaning they can effortlessly swim into shoals of fish to catch prey at shallower depths than other diving fish-eaters. The downside is that their feathers are not waterproof, so when they leave the water, they have to dry off. This is why you often see cormorants standing with their wings open after they leave the water.

→ River Trent wetlands.

LOWER REACHES

← Otters have a thick waterproof outer layer of fur.

↓ This camera trap can be left in the field for months, recording which species pass by.

Otters have the densest fur of any mammal, with 50,000 hairs per cm². Eurasian otters have two layers of fur, with a thick, waterproof outer layer and a warm inner layer. The inner coat's high density of hairs trap air bubbles to create a heat-insulating layer. This fur allows otters to continue to hunt in water in the winter. To dry off they will rub themselves on vegetation and retreat to the holt (their nest) to dry off undercover.

Camera traps

Camera traps have never been more widely available and can be fairly affordable. Although they may seem a bit advanced, most are pretty user-friendly and can offer a peek into the lives of many secretive and nocturnal animals.

The first thing to do is to find a place that is safe to leave the camera trap, ideally away from public footpaths. If on private land, seek the landowner's permission before leaving the camera out.

Some camera traps can last for months in the field, so decide how long you want to leave it and make sure the memory card is empty and the battery is full. I like to find a trail that animals have made and leave the trap near there.

Depending on what I'm hoping to catch on camera, I might put some food by the trap as well.

Many models come with a strap to tie to a tree, or you can screw them into a spike that goes in the ground. You can adjust sensitivity, increasing it if you want footage of smaller mammals, or decreasing it when you might want larger animals like badgers or foxes. A camera trap is a brilliant way to learn more about the behaviour and patterns of animals in a particular area – what species are present, what time they are active and how many are in the area. It's such a useful piece of kit, and reviewing the footage it has captured is always exciting – you never know what you might discover.

Wildlife photography

Now that most smartphones come with a decent camera, wildlife photography has never been more popular. What better way to see and document the wildlife you encounter?

While we may tend to picture someone in full camo, toting a lens longer than a French baguette, the reality is that it's a hobby open to all kinds of people with different skill sets. Rivers are a great place to start photographing wildlife as the water attracts many species who come to rivers to drink and find food.

Long-lens photography certainly has its place for getting images of more skittish species like kingfisher, otter and dipper without disturbing them. Macro (close-up) photography, on the other hand, is a window to a whole other world, and allows you to explore the smallest details of plants, insects and fungi along the river. Or why not take a wider view and photograph the river itself? This is especially rewarding if you can return to the same spot throughout the seasons. I tend to operate in two ways: I either travel light and walk as much of the river as possible, seeing what I can find, or hunker down in one spot with a tripod and see what comes to me.

TOP TIPS FOR WILDLIFE PHOTOGRAPHY

- **Get as close to the subject as you can without disturbing it,** especially on a smartphone. Avoid zooming in as this will decrease the quality of the image. It's important to note that no photo is worth disturbing the animal, so only go as close as you feel the animal is comfortable.
- **Get low down** for a different perspective. Often the images will look better if taken at the animal's level.
- When using a long lens, remember to **keep the shutter speed above the focal length** in millimetres of the lens, e.g. if it's a 300mm lens, make sure your shutter speed is over 1/300th of a second to keep the images nice and sharp.
- **The best camera is the one in your hand!** Don't worry too much about getting the most expensive model. Also consider second-hand kit to get more for your money.
- **Learn about the subject** you want to photograph beforehand. An awareness of the species' typical behaviour can go a long way towards helping you get some good images.

→ Placing river critters in a fish tank on location means they can be quickly released back into the river after taking a few pictures.

River aquarium

If you're looking to collect invertebrates while river dipping, one of the best ways to view them is in your own river aquarium, filled with river water. A glass one looks best in my opinion but plastic ones also work well. The tank should be placed away from direct sunlight and a lid is a good idea to stop any critter jumping out. Make sure you decorate the tank with rocks, sunken logs and plants that would be found in the invertebrates' natural environment. I quite like using *Vallisneria*, as it waves and flows in the tank. If you are intending to keep the animals for more than a couple of days, then a filter is necessary to replicate the flow of the river and cycle oxygen.

As long as the species you are collecting isn't protected, like white-clawed crayfish or medicinal leech for example, there's no harm in collecting them to view in an aquarium. If it's a species that demands high oxygen levels, like most river flies, it's better to put it back after a quick look. Other species, such as shrimps, will thrive in a tank.

I tend to keep various species for a month or two before releasing them back into where they came from, and this is an invaluable way of learning about habits and behaviour. For me, as a photographer, it also allows me to take some lovely close-up images.

It's important that you don't mix animals from different waterways in the same tank, or when releasing them back into the wild, as you may introduce diseases and parasites by accident. If you aren't confident about whether the species will be OK in the tank, it's best to release it and just enjoy it in the moment by the river.

THINGS TO KNOW

- **Keep the aquarium as cool as possible** by keeping it in a cool room or basement. Between 15°C and 18°C is ideal. Failing that, you may require a chiller for the summer months.
- **Don't overcrowd the aquarium.** Less is more, to avoid the animals becoming stressed.
- **Water changes are needed** about once a month, and you should clean out the filter every couple of weeks.
- **Pond snails, hog lice and *Gammarus* shrimps** are good invertebrates to collect as they will thrive in a tank.

Where to visit

ATTENBOROUGH NATURE RESERVE, Nottingham

This large Nottinghamshire Wildlife Trust reserve covers 145 hectares of mixed wetland, woodland, scrub and river to create an oasis for wildlife. Formerly a gravel pit, it is now a vital area for migratory birds and insects, and a refuge for many fish species including spined loach. The River Trent runs at the back of the reserve and the River Erewash also empties into the lakes on site.

Although Sir David Attenborough officially opened the reserve in 1966, it is not actually named after him. Rather, the name comes from the village where the reserve is located. In a strange twist, however, David Attenborough's family are originally from the area and so his family may well be named after the village as well.

The reserve has fantastic facilities, with ample parking, a large café, wildlife hides and easy terrain for all abilities to walk around. The nature centre has a terrace that overlooks the lakes, where you can enjoy a cuppa with a chance of a kingfisher flying by. It has a sand martin bank built into an island at the back of the centre. In summer, this is full of life as sand martins nest in the holes next to the hide.

There are various routes you can take around the reserve, with most being circular, ranging up to a few miles. Some can get quite muddy in the winter, and the back path by the Trent can be busy with cyclists.

In the winter, many ducks visit the site with wigeon, teal and shoveler making up the bulk. In the spring and summer, it's renowned for its warblers with grasshopper, sedge, reed and Cetti's warbler all present. And it's not just birds: the reserve is home to many dragonfly and damselfly species, including banded demoiselle, emerald and small red-eyed damselfly, emperor dragonfly and brown, migrant and southern hawkers.

LOWER REACHES

YNYS-HIR, Powys

Managed by the RSPB, Ynys-hir is nestled in Powys with the Dyfi flowing through the northern edge of the reserve. As well as the wetland, it has a myriad of habitats including Welsh oak woodland, estuary salt marsh, lowland wet grasslands, freshwater pools, reedbeds and peat bog. In Welsh, *ynys-hir* means 'long island', which refers to a wooded ridge which was once surrounded by marshland.

With 800 hectares to choose from, there's plenty of room to find your own corner to spot species such as waders, ducks and herons. The oakwoods support all the characteristic birds of broadleaved woodland, including pied flycatcher, redstart, wood warbler and both great and lesser spotted woodpeckers. Spring is best for the flycatchers and redstarts, which will be nesting at this time, while winter is best for the woodpeckers, when there are fewer leaves to hide behind. Birds of prey can be seen throughout the year and include red kites, hen harriers, merlins and peregrines. Non-native conifers have been planted over the years for timber and are slowly being phased out in favour of natives, although they are preferred by goldcrests and coal tits and, in winter, attract crossbills.

Twenty-six species of butterfly have been recorded on the reserve, including clouded yellows, as well as clearwings, which are rarer day-flying moths. The many wildflowers attract these insects, as well as the rarer species of plants that can be found, such as sundew, bog asphodel and bog rosemary.

As with many RSPB reserves, the usual facilities are all available, with parking (free for RSPB members), toilets and a café. There are five hides on site to allow a look over various habitats. The visitor centre has a picnic area outside and lots of information on species that have been seen recently. A mixture of walking routes are available, from the green trail, which is a mile long, to the red route, which is about three miles long.

HAM WALL, Somerset

This RSPB reserve really is the jewel in the Somerset Levels' crown, with an expansive 260 hectares of wetland. 'Ham' is an old term for pasture or meadow, and the Ham Wall may have been a bank to hold water on the flooded fields. One of the key species that the RSPB hoped to encourage on the wetland was the bittern (see also page 69), which over the last century has seen a resurgence in numbers. In 2023, between 40 and 50 males were recorded 'booming' (a loud, foghorn-like call given to proclaim territory) on the site during the breeding season, showing that the species is thriving in the area.

One possible reason for the bitterns' success is the unofficial introduction of Perez frogs, which are native to the Iberian Peninsula. Likely a release from pet owners, they are now well established in the Levels. Another non-native species which, much like the Perez frog, is becoming food for many species is the sunbleak – a small silverfish introduced via the aquarium trade. Although, the release of non-native species is generally considered to have a negative impact on native wildlife, for the bitterns and other heron species the frogs have proved a useful food source. Other notable birds found on the reserve include bearded tits, marsh harriers and garganeys.

There is a car park (free for RSPB members) with an information point and staff on hand who can let you know what has been sighted recently. Toilets are also on site, as well as a stall offering hot drinks and snacks. There are two hides, two viewing platforms and eight screens, all of which are usually open from dawn until dusk.

The reserve boasts over three miles of trails, all with regular seating. The main track is wide with a raised hard surface, and is a local cycle path. Ham Wall Loop has bike gates to prevent access to motorbikes, but they are wide enough to accommodate most wheelchairs.

INSH MARSHES, Speyside

Insh Marshes covers 10km² of the River Spey floodplain. Once intensively grazed, this area has been managed by the RSPB since 1975, creating a large wetland area where many species now thrive. It's a popular spot for tourists in the Highlands. The Spey enters at Kincraig, creating Loch Insh, and empties at Farr. Insh Marshes acts like a giant sponge, absorbing excess water, which helps to stop the flooding downstream of places like Aviemore. At its capacity, it can hold 35 million m³ of water. That's the same as 1,400 Olympic swimming pools!

The marshes are home to large populations of breeding waders, including curlews, lapwings, redshanks and snipe. Lots of waterfowl are also present, with whooper swans overwintering, and goldeneye breeding in the summer. Arctic charr are found in the deeper parts of the marshes and travel into the Spey to spawn in the winter.

One of the best times to visit the reserve is in October to see it in its full autumnal glory. The banks are lined with birch, aspen and oak, which showcase a mixture of golds, yellows and reds when the leaves are about to fall. There are many trails to walk along the reserve, including the three-mile-long Invertromie trail, which offers views of the surrounding moorland (note that the ground can be soft and uneven). There are also guided walks during the spring and summer, with a chance of seeing a multitude of species including osprey, crested tits and red squirrels.

There are two hides on site to allow you to view wildlife undercover and a picnic area if you want to enjoy some outdoor dining in the summer.

It's free to visit, but donations are encouraged to help with the upkeep of the site.

Species spotlight

EUROPEAN POND TURTLE *Emys orbicularis*

It may surprise you to learn that we once had a native freshwater turtle in Britain – the European pond turtle. It hasn't been here in any numbers for around 4,000 years, but there is a movement to try and reintroduce it to some of its former range in England. A cooling climate a few thousand years ago is likely to have been a factor in its extinction, and it was also hunted by humans, as turtle remains have been found in human settlements dating back 6,000 years. Despite rumours of these turtles' presence on the Norfolk Broads well into the nineteenth century, it's probable that these were released pets rather than glacial relics.

The European pond turtle is not a large turtle, the length of the shell is generally around 20cm, with females the larger of the sexes. Compared to North American turtles and terrapins, its colour is a little subdued; it is mostly black, but can have some spattering of yellow on the top and more on the bottom of the carapace (upper shell).

To lay her eggs, the female pond turtle climbs onto land, sometimes moving considerable distances to find a suitable area, with sandy banks being ideal. She will lay up to 18 eggs, with the young hatching out a few months later and heading for water.

HORSEFLY *Tabanidae spp.*

There are 30 species of horsefly in the UK, and the unlucky amongst us will know them for their rather painful bite. Only the female bites as she needs the protein from mammal blood to help her eggs develop. The males drink mostly nectar from flowers. The female lays her eggs on damp soil where the larvae will search for other invertebrates to feed on.

At only around 1cm long, most horsefly species aren't especially large, but they pack a powerful bite. The jaws act like a chainsaw and cut into flesh. They lack the anaesthetic saliva of mosquitos, so you feel every nibble of these insects. They do, however, release an anticoagulant, which stops your blood clotting and provides an easy way for the female horsefly to lap up her meal.

The most striking thing about these blood suckers is their incredible compound eyes, in some cases a colourful mosaic of greens, burgundy and yellows for which you can almost forgive them for making a meal of you!

CHINESE WATER DEER *Hydropotes inermis*

We have six species of deer in Britain, and yet only two are native. It's probably no surprise that the Chinese water deer is one of the non-natives. This strange and beautiful mammal was first kept at London Zoo in 1873, but several individuals escaped from its sister zoo, Whipsnade, in 1929.

Numbers increased through introductions into deer parks and subsequent escapes and releases, and the British population is now thought to account for 10 per cent of the world's total. Because of the proximity of some of these introductions (and escapes) to the Norfolk Broads and Cambridgeshire fens, it soon became established there, with an estimated population of 2,100. The fenland of southern England was a perfect substitute for their native home in the wetlands of eastern and central China and Korea. Overall the shape and body is typical of a deer, though they lack antlers and instead the males have large tusks, which they use to fight during the rut in winter. Their pale fawn fur and distinctly round ears help distinguish them from any other deer in Britain.

Not as social as other deer species, they are normally alone or in pairs. Unlike another smaller Asian deer species, the muntjac, they are not particularly damaging to the environment, as they are more fussy in their choice of food, sticking to large wetland areas where they feed mostly on the reeds.

BURBOT *Lota lota*

This fish is the only member of the cod family to live in fresh water and was once relatively common in England's east-flowing rivers, from South Yorkshire to East Anglia. It has the sad distinction to be the last vertebrate to go extinct in England, with the last confirmed sighting in 1969 in the Great Ouse in Cambridge. There are currently plans to reintroduce it back to East Anglia.

The reason for its disappearance is a combination of bad water quality and loss of access to the floodplains where it liked to spawn. Being a brown, mottled bottom-dweller, the burbot may lack the glamour of other lost species such as lynxes and wolves, but that doesn't mean it shouldn't come back and indeed thrive.

There is a lot of misinformation about burbot, with classic arguments claiming they can only spawn under ice and that our rivers are too polluted and warm for them to survive. Both of these lines of reasoning are nonsense. Burbot ideally like to spawn in river margins around 4°C but can hatch young in temperatures up to 7°C. A feasibility study performed by the University of Southampton found that water quality and habitat in select areas of the burbot's previous range were sufficient for reintroduction. The River Wissey in Norfolk is currently the favoured choice.

BITTERN *Botaurus stellaris*

Outwardly, it's just a brown heron, but to many birdwatchers across the UK, the bittern is the holy grail of wetland birding. Numbers of bitterns have fluctuated wildly over the years. It was a fairly common breeding bird until the late nineteenth century, when it became extinct due to a mixture of hunting and loss of wetland habitat. It then returned on its own, and by the 1950s there were thought to be an estimated 100 birds in the country, before the population crashed in the 1990s to just 10 breeding males. Currently the outlook looks much more positive, with an estimated 227 pairs.

The bittern has the typical heron shape, though with a more hunched posture, and a mix of browns and blacks help it blend into its favoured reedbed habitat. Once the bittern skulks behind some reeds, it is incredibly difficult to spot. The male has a loud call to attract a mate, called 'booming'.

Counting booming males allows us to estimate bittern numbers without seeing them. I once stood close to a reedbed at Dungeness in Kent and a bittern started booming a few metres from me. I could feel the reverberations in my ribcage!

COMMON REED *Phragmites australis*

The beating heart of many wetlands in Britain is the reedbed, formed by stands of this tall, water-loving grass species. Many creatures rely on this valuable habitat. Reeds produce fresh green growth in the spring, which many waterfowl will gleefully devour, while in the winter they turn a golden brown colour which, if you are there at sunset, looks incredible.

Common reeds flower from August to October, producing clustered heads of small purplish flowers. The seeds from common reeds are an important food source for reed bunting, bearded tit and many other small birds. The reeds will also spread via rhizomes and creep across the shallow water.

The plants as a whole can grow up to 4m tall and are a vital part of wetlands and lower reaches on rivers. They act as a buffer to wave erosion so are often planted in areas with water sports and heavy boat traffic to help prevent the banks falling in. Their submerged parts provide important nurseries for many fish and invertebrates. Their most famous use historically was in the construction of thatched housing, where parts of the reeds would be cut down and placed on the roofs. More recently, the hollow stems are being used as eco-friendly straws.

WATER MINT *Mentha aquatica*

Like its terrestrial cousin, water mint has a strong aromatic scent and is often used in cooking. Its herbal uses include treating stomach aches and calming nerves, as it is a mild sedative.

The plant itself has a stem that can reach up to 90cm tall, with rows of pale oval green leaves. It flowers from July to October, with groupings of purple flowers at the top. It readily hybridises with other members of the mint family and, if crossed with spearmint, will produce the sterile hybrid plant of peppermint.

Water mint is widespread across Great Britain in wet meadows, bogs and riverbanks, being found both on the land and in the water. It is a larval food plant of the aptly named mint moth, which can be seen flying around in the daytime looking for clumps of mint to lay its eggs on. Not exclusive to water mint, it can be found on most members of the mint family and can be seen in quite large numbers. For a small moth no bigger than 1cm in wingspan, it's actually quite a pretty insect, with purples, yellows and whites on its wings.

SWALLOWTAIL BUTTERFLY *Papilio machaon*

This stunning creature is the largest butterfly in Great Britain, with a wingspan of 9cm. The adult has a mix of yellows, blues, reds and blacks on the tops of the wings, as well as long 'tails' on the hindwings, which are reminiscent of a swallow's tail streamers, earning it its name. With its large size and unique shape and colouration, it is not really confusable with any other species in Britain. The full-grown caterpillars are arguably just as magnificent: vibrant green with orange and black bands across them. However, they start off black and white to mimic bird droppings and so avoid detection by predators.

Although the species is widespread across Europe, the English subspecies *britannicus* is confined to the Norfolk Broads. This is partly due to the distribution of the sole larval food plant, milk-parsley. Because the food plant is found mostly in wet habitats, this butterfly is primarily associated with large wetland and slow-moving rivers.

Historically, the swallowtail had a wider distribution across southern England, but with the drainage of wetlands in the eighteenth century, it just managed to hold on in Norfolk.

In a good season there may be two broods, with adults emerging in May until early July, and then again in August, with any caterpillars overwintering in a waterproof chrysalis.

The continental subspecies, which is far less fussy in its diet habits and feeds on most kinds of umbellifers, does occasionally turn up in Britain. With warming temperatures, it's thought that this butterfly could colonise England and potentially hybridise with the British subspecies. While they look very similar, the continental race is not as vibrantly coloured.

BEARDED TIT *Panurus biarmicus*

A reedbed specialist, this striking bird isn't actually a tit but the sole member of a distinct family, Panuridae. It is therefore sometimes known as bearded reedling instead. The name issues don't stop there, however, as the bird doesn't really have anything resembling a beard, although the males do have long black bands from the eyes down to the chin that look more like a handlebar moustache, which contrasts with their otherwise light blue-grey heads.

Females are less flashy and are mostly brown, lacking the grey head and moustache. Both sexes have a long, graduated tail, and black and white markings on their brown wings. The colouration of these birds means they blend into the reeds perfectly and often the only sign of their presence is their call, which sounds like a rather dry, metallic 'ping', given in chorus by a flock on the move.

They spend most of their lives in large reedbeds, feeding on seeds in the winter and insects during the summer. To help with this coarse diet of seeds, these birds will routinely eat small stones, which grind the seeds in their stomachs and help to break them down.

When it comes to nesting season, the female builds a nest out of piles of dead reed stems. As they are seldom alone, if you are lucky enough to spot one, you will often see loose groups of them.

GREAT CRESTED GREBE *Podiceps cristatus*

Easily my favourite British bird, the great crested grebe is a must-see for any springtime birdwatcher. Often associated with still waters, they are also at home in large slow-moving rivers. From February, they begin their courtship ritual, which usually involves calling, synchronised swimming, preening, fanning out their feathery ruffs, head shaking, and finally the weed dance. This is where the couple hold tufts of water weed in their bills and stand up in the water, chest to chest. If the female is suitably impressed, they will pair up.

During the breeding season, the male and female look pretty much identical, with a crested head and an orange ruff around the cheeks They have white faces, a dark cap, a white neck and a dark body. In the winter, the crest and ruff disappear and they look more monochrome. The chicks, nicknamed 'humbugs', have black and white stripes.

When small, the chicks will often sit on a parent's back. To help them digest the many fish they eat, the parents will feed them feathers. This is thought to help slow down digestion and allow more time for the fish bones to dissolve.

5

The Estuary

As the river nears the end of its journey and meets the sea, we can discover a borderland of species at the estuary, with the river bringing a huge amount of nutrients to the marine environment. The river is now quite turbid and full of detritus with little clarity, and the riverbed is thick mud.

The biggest influence is the mix of saline and fresh water. This brackish water is in constant flux depending on the tides and weather. Due to the higher density of salt water, the fresh water is generally closest to the surface, with the saltier water underneath it. Further out to sea, the fresh water is diluted and eventually becomes completely saline.

Very few fish species can traverse both types of water, and the stress it causes their body will often kill less specialised fish. Salmon, eels and brown trout are the best-known examples of species that can mix between the two. In certain areas, if the right mix of salt and fresh water is present, you can find completely marine species such as common gobies mixing with freshwater species such as barbel.

← Mawddach Estuary, Gwynedd, Wales.

Mud!

With this being the final stop for any debris leaving the river, all the mud, sediment and detritus eventually ends up here. The sediment falls out of the surface layer into the denser, saltier layer of water moving into the estuary. As it drops, it gets trapped and accumulates on the bottom. Slowly, the estuary grows muddier and muddier, and shallower and shallower.

This mud may look rather devoid of life, but it is quite the opposite. It will have species such as bristle worms, bivalves and mud snails tucked away beneath the surface while the tide is out, who will then poke back up when the water returns. Many crustaceans also live in the mud, such as brown shrimp, which burrow into the mud to find food. It has been estimated that the shellfish and worms found in a single cubic metre of estuary mud can contain as many calories as 16 chocolate bars. It's no wonder, then, that so many migratory birds flock to Britain's estuaries each winter to feed and find shelter in the relatively ice-free coastal areas.

Quicksand

You might only be familiar with it from Saturday morning cartoons, but quicksand is, in fact, real, and is present in several locations in Britain. Hotspots include Morecambe Bay in north-west England, Camber Sands in Sussex and Crantock Beach in Cornwall.

Quicksand is a mixture of water and fine granular material, such as sand, silt or clay, which behaves like a liquid. It forms when the sand is saturated with water and then agitated, causing the water to become trapped and the sand to lose its strength.

I should point out that, although you should be careful, it's rarely as life-threatening as the cartoons suggest. If you find yourself in quicksand, spread your weight and try slow back-and-forth movements to loosen the sand.

Tides

Great Britain has a wealth of large estuaries, including the Severn Estuary, which has the largest tidal range in Europe, at up to 15m. The tide's influence on our coastline has ebbed and flowed over the years (sorry, couldn't help myself). In many areas of Britain we have put in weirs to hold back the tide further upstream, so the tides in these places would previously have extended much further inland. The weirs have stopped many creatures that spend time in the ocean from penetrating further inland, severely hampering the breeding efforts of fish such as shad, smelt, lamprey and sturgeon, all of which have suffered declines because they need to breed in fresh water.

One of the most spectacular sights you can see on a British river is a tidal bore. This is when a surge of water races back up the river from the sea, caused by a combination of a rising tide and the physical shape of the estuary. The sea water is pushed towards the surface and creates a continuous wave. There are only around 100 rivers in the world with a bore, and 20 of them can

← It may look plain, however, mud is full of invertebrates that feed many of the birds that live in estuaries.

be found in Britain. They include the Trent, Mersey, Dee and, the most dramatic and famous, the Severn. The Severn Bore can reach 2m high and run at a speed of 12mph. With up to 250 bores a year, there are plenty of chances to see one but only a few in the spring and autumn grow to their maximum size. It often attracts a crowd, with some people even surfing it!

End of the line

Marking the end of the road for the river, the estuary is a dumping ground, not only for natural material but many human-made items as well. All manner of litter, waste and debris gets washed downstream, from microplastics to car tyres. In the estuary itself, you also get build-ups of discarded fishing nets from commercial outfits.

Estuaries are a magnet for many fish species and attract people wanting to net these fish. The trouble is that they are messy places with sunken trees and all kinds of obstacles in the water that can catch and snag a net. When these nets are broken off, they become 'ghost' nets, still catching and killing wildlife even though they won't be brought in. It's estimated that ghost gear makes up at least 10 per cent of marine litter. This roughly translates to between 500,000 and 1 million tonnes of fishing gear abandoned in the ocean globally each year.

↑ The Severn Bore at Minsterworth, Gloucestershire.
↓ Litter on the River Lea.

There's no clear solution, but reporting lost gear can help as it may be possible to retrieve it safely at a later date. The design of the nets used should be appropriate for the terrain to help avoid losses, and old nets should be recycled rather than simply dumped in the sea.

Elvermen

There is a tradition of catching elvers (young eels) in many British rivers. Today, the River Severn is the epicentre of this practice. The Severn acts like a giant funnel, collecting huge numbers of elvers when they are travelling on the Gulf Stream towards Europe, and so has the largest numbers of eels returning to it of any British river.

For hundreds of years, people have caught the little elvers in handmade, fine mesh nets, which are left in the water in the dead of night. Every so often, the nets are checked and the elvers are emptied into a bucket. These young eels are a delicacy in Asia and across Europe and can fetch huge prices. Today, on the legal market, elvers cost around £150 per kg, but on the black market they can cost up to £4,000 per kg.

This may sound like all take and no give, involving a species now classed globally as Critically Endangered, but many of the 'elvermen' have signed up to a programme in which they donate some of their catch to be released over barriers that the eels would otherwise struggle to pass, allowing them to access regions where there are fewer eels and so helping to boost numbers upstream. Some elvermen also visit aquariums to teach school children about eels before the elvers are eventually released.

Hides

The estuary is often an open and flat environment, which means getting close to the wildlife there can be tricky. However, many nature reserves have solved this problem by installing hides.

Essentially, these are small wooden buildings with gaps at the front to allow you to view wildlife, most often birds, without spooking them. Some viewing slots are sealed glass, but others have a window that can be opened, and these are my preferred kind for taking photos. If they have a ledge on the window, I like to take a clamp with a tripod attachment, which saves me carrying a tripod around. You can fix a spotting scope or camera to the clamp.

It can be very rewarding waiting for that special rarity, maybe a long-billed dowitcher or a purple heron, to turn up. Seating can be a little rough, so if you are in it for the long haul, it doesn't hurt to bring a small cushion and, in the winter, a hot drink in a flask is a comfort. Staying still in a hide for hours can get chilly!

Mudlarking

A mudlarker is someone who scavenges along the banks of a river for items of value and historical worth. It's particularly popular near large rivers in cities, as this is where items lost

← Hides provide an opportunity to see birds that might normally be shy.

↑ Mudlarking finds from the River Thames, London.

or discarded by people are most likely to turn up.

The Thames in London is perhaps the capital for mudlarking. As this was once the biggest and busiest port in the world, and has had settlements along its banks for the past 2,000 years, many things have inevitably been thrown in the water over the centuries. Common finds include clay pipes, bits of pottery and thimbles, but rarer finds have included Roman hairpins, medieval gold rings and mammoth bones.

If you want to try mudlarking on the tidal Thames, it's relatively easy. You need to hold a current foreshore permit from the Port of London Authority (PLA) if you're going out on your own, but there are various guided tours you can join, which are great for beginners.

Crabbing

You can't beat a bit of crabbing, and many a child has spent a summer holiday collecting buckets of

MUDLARKING TIPS AND RULES

- **Wellingtons are a must** as the clue is in the name: it's going to get muddy! **Gloves are also a good idea** to avoid cutting fingertips.
- Any gold, silver, or objects of possible **historical significance (more than 300 years old) need to be reported** to the relevant authority.
- Often there are no steps or slipway down to the foreshore so make sure there's public access to get down there. **Don't climb walls or trespass to get to it.**
- If you want to try mudlarking in London, be aware that **permits are only valid west of the Thames Barrier** and make sure to familiarise yourself with the various location restrictions.

↑ Crabbing at Fowey Harbour, Cornwall.

crabs. Estuaries are full of crabs as the murky water and mud provide ample habitat. To find the perfect crabbing spot, look for somewhere with deeper water that's ideally not dry at low tide. Piers, harbour walls and jetties are all good choices.

The equipment is pretty simple. The basic version is a piece of meat attached to a rope, which you lower into the water. When you feel a pull, gently pull the crab up and put it into a bucket filled with sea water. Some traps now have a net, which offers a higher success rate.

Crabs aren't fussy; champion crabbers hold bacon as the prime crab bait, but I've always gone with scraps from the fishmongers. Green shore crabs are normally the first to come along but you could also catch prawns, edible crabs and, if you're unlucky, a velvet swimming crab, which are best avoided as they love nothing more than clamping onto a finger!

It's important not to keep the crabs in the bucket for more than a couple of hours and to release them where you caught them after admiring them.

TOP TIPS FOR CRABBING

- **It's easy enough to make your own crabbing equipment:** save some money and simply tie some bacon, fish or any scraps you have to a piece of thin rope and lower it down.
- **You can buy eco-friendly crab lines** made of a hemp line and wooden handle, which is what I'd suggest using if you're not making your own.
- **The best time to go crabbing is when the tide is coming in.**
- **Don't overfill the bucket.** Once you've caught a few crabs, release them and, if you want to carry on, just put some fresh sea water in and start again.
- When you are done with the crab line, please **dispose of it responsibly** by binning it or, better yet, giving it to another person to use. Many harbours are littered with discarded crab lines.

Where to visit

DONNA NOOK, Lincolnshire

Donna Nook is nestled between the Humber estuary and the Wash estuary, meaning two things are in abundance here: mud and biodiversity.

Lincolnshire Wildlife Trust manages a section, allowing the public to see one of the highest numbers of grey seals in the country. Each November and December the grey seals come onto the mudflats to give birth and visitors can get a fantastic view of these creatures. The Trust offers 'pupdates' on its website each year to let people know the numbers of seals present and how many pups have been born.

There are around six miles of coastline to explore and, as well as the seals, the area is home to many birds, salt marsh plants and insects. Plant life includes sea-buckthorn, whose berries attract large numbers of fieldfare, redwing and starling in the winter.

It's a short walk from the car park and access is level, along a sandy footpath. With the seals being so close, binoculars aren't essential, but worth taking to view the full scope of the colony and to spot other wildlife. If you're lucky, you may see a seal pup that is jet black – only around one in 400 are born like this and the rest are pure white.

There is normally a van selling food in the car park, as well as a few portable toilets in the peak seal season (the rest of the year there are none). It can get very busy at weekends during this time. Dogs aren't permitted on site, to avoid disturbance to the seals. There is a fence to allow the seals some peace, but part of the area is also Ministry of Defence land used for target bombing, so best not to wander out! The area has historical significance, with remnants of Second World War defences and a radar station.

THE ESTUARY

THAMES ESTUARY, City of London

Most people don't associate London with the coast, which is 50 miles away, but the sea's influence is very evident on the Thames. The tides push right up until Teddington, making the whole of the London Thames tidal.

Harbour seals are fairly common closer to the estuary, and even sharks such as tope and smoothhound enjoy the muddy water to hunt small fish. As many as 125 species of fish have been recorded in the Thames, with the majority of them being found in the estuary. They support a wide range of fish-eating birds and other predators. In 2006, a northern bottlenose whale even made it up the river as far as Battersea, although it eventually died and the bones were donated to the Natural History Museum.

Walking routes are all fairly easy, with paths running along the majority of the Thames and suitable for all abilities. Access right to the riverside can be a little trickier but there are certain points where you can get to the shore at low tide. The tide can creep up quickly so it's best to go in groups and be aware of the tide table.

To avoid the risk of flooding in central London and to help with large high tides, the Thames Barrier was completed in 1982. Spanning 520m across the River Thames near Woolwich, it is the second-largest retractable flood defence barrier in the world. The barrier has 10 steel gates that, when raised, are about as high as a five-storey building. Each gate weighs approximately 3,000 tonnes and is designed to withstand an overall load of about 9,000 tonnes of water. When the barrier is fully raised, it creates a solid steel wall that stops water from flowing upstream towards the city.

SOLWAY FIRTH, Cumbria / Dumfries and Galloway

The Solway Firth is located off the west coast of Britain, between Dumfries and Galloway in Scotland and Cumbria in England. It's part of the Solway Coast Area of Outstanding Natural Beauty (AONB), designated for its scenic and ecological value. A firth is a narrow inlet of the sea, or the estuary of a river, and is a term used particularly in Scotland. The word 'firth' comes from the Old Norse word *fjörthr*, which means 'fjord'.

The Rivers Eden and Esk flow into the Solway Firth, along with several smaller rivers. In England, it's based on soft sandstone, while the Scottish side is made of harder granite rocks, giving the landscape a more rugged feel. It is the third-largest estuary in Britain and a magnet for migrating birds such as whooper swans, pink-footed geese and curlews. The concentrations of smaller birds and of rodents attract birds of prey such as peregrine falcons, short-eared owls and the beautiful hen harrier.

Other notable species of the Solway include allis shad (an Atlantic fish species), Baltic tellin (a small saltwater clam) and the natterjack toad. These little toads prefer coastal dune habitats, and the Solway is home to over 10 per cent of the total British population.

The Solway Coast is a huge area, spanning more than 110 square miles, with a number of paths to choose from; Crosscanonby Carr, Campfield Marsh RSPB Reserve, Finglandrigg Woods, Glasson Moss and Watchtree Nature Reserve all have routes. Some notable beaches include Silloth, known for its sandy shoreline and views of the Lake District, and the quieter stretches around Bowness-on-Solway.

There are many activities to enjoy in the area, from hiking to paddle boarding, and its long coastline is also popular for horse riding. When the tide is out, you can cover an area stretching from Maryport to Silloth, with places to stop along the way. The area is also recognised for its dark skies, making it an excellent location for stargazing and enjoying the night sky away from city lights.

RSPB CONWY, Llandudno

This area on the Conwy estuary, just south of Llandudno, has undergone a remarkable transformation. Having once been used as a dumpsite for waste material from the A55 tunnel, it is now a 46-hectare RSPB reserve offering views of Snowdonia.

The River Conwy flows into the Irish Sea right next to the reserve, which features a range of diverse habitats including salt marshes, mudflats and freshwater wetlands. The estuary is interwoven with a couple of large lagoons and various islands. These are always worth scanning to see which birds are resting up on them.

More than 220 species of bird have been seen on the reserve, from rare migrants like alpine swift to the residents like little grebes. However, it is best known for its spectacular starling murmurations in the winter, with thousands of birds utilising the reedbeds to roost in at night. It's best to go in the evening to see this spectacle, as this is when the starlings start to return. If a bird of prey, such as a sparrowhawk, is harassing the starlings, you'll get an even better view as they swoop around to avoid the predator.

There are also plenty of interesting plants here, including orchids such as the rare *coccinea* subspecies of early marsh-orchid, and the bee orchid. The freshwater ponds and lakes are also home to multiple dragonfly and damselfly species, including black darter – the only dragonfly species in the UK that is black, the males are mostly black with yellow stripes whereas the females are more yellow.

Several trails around the reserve link up the various habitats, ranging from walks of under a mile to a couple of miles. They are all on fairly level ground and you can follow a circular route. There are four hides with adjacent viewing screens, and five additional viewing screens, all with variable height viewing slots.

Other facilities include a free car park and a visitor centre with a café and toilets.

Species spotlight

STARRY SMOOTH-HOUND *Mustelus asterias*

Smooth-hounds are small sharks often found near river mouths. They can't survive in fresh water, needing saline to live, but the nutrients and mud around estuaries mean there is a plentiful supply of crabs and small fish, which the smooth-hounds feed on. It was previously thought that we had two species in Britain, the common and starry smooth-hound, but genetic analysis of over 800 fish found them all to be starry smooth-hounds. Although one of the key features of starry smooth-hounds is the presence of spots, not all of them have spots, so the two species are very difficult to tell apart without genetic tests.

Smooth-hounds are so named due to their distinctively smooth skin texture. Unlike many other sharks that have rough, sandpaper-like skin covered with tiny scales called dermal denticles, smooth-hounds have a softer, more streamlined appearance. This smoothness helps them reduce drag as they swim through the water, making them efficient hunters. They don't have sharp teeth like other sharks and instead have hardened gums for crushing prey, leading to their other name: gummy sharks.

OSPREY *Pandion haliaetus*

Rivers are important migratory routes for ospreys, which tend to arrive on British shores around March, having flown north from their wintering grounds in West Africa. The reason for this long migration is plentiful food, longer daylight hours for hunting and fewer predators of their chicks than in the south. Ospreys can live for more than 20 years, repeating the long migration each year. Hitting estuaries first, they follow the river inland until they find a suitable nest site, such as a large loch, lake or reservoir. Ospreys build large nests, using sticks, seaweed and other materials. They typically return to the same nest year after year, adding to it each season.

The osprey is brown on top and white below, with a white head and dark band across its eyes, making it a distinctive bird of prey. These magnificent birds are known for their spectacular diving technique, hovering above the water before diving feet-first to catch fish. When the talons hit the fish, they lock down into the flesh and carry it to a nearby branch to feed on.

Ospreys faced significant declines due to pesticide use in the mid-twentieth century, becoming a rare sight. However, conservation efforts, including banning harmful pesticides and protecting nesting sites, have helped their populations recover in recent years.

SMELT *Osmerus eperlanus*

For many fish, the estuary is just a stop-off point on the journey up or downstream, but for European smelt, it's a year-round home. The murky water helps them hide from predators and the habitat is rich in their prey, including small fish and invertebrates.

When they need to spawn, these slender silver fish push upstream into fresh water and find an area with a gravelly bed. This normally happens at night. The female attaches the eggs to the riverbed and the male fertilises them.

The smelt's lower jaw projects beyond the upper jaw, and the mouth is lined with rows of many teeth used to grip small prey. They have clear fins, including an adipose fin (a small fin behind the dorsal fin), indicating their shared ancestry with salmon, which also have this. Smelt have the unusual distinction of having a strong smell of cucumber, which can become more pronounced during spawning.

Smelt were once far more common in Britain, found as far inland as Nottingham, but weirs, sluices and barriers to migration have greatly impacted them, restricting them to a fraction of their former range.

EUROPEAN EEL *Anguilla anguilla*

The eel has astounded humanity for millennia. The ancient Egyptians associated eels with the sun god Atum and believed they sprang to life when the sun warmed the Nile. In the fourth century BC, Aristotle proclaimed that eels spontaneously generated within 'the entrails of the earth'.

We now know much more about the eels' life cycle. They spend several years fattening themselves up in fresh water and then head to the Sargasso Sea to spawn and then die. However, there are still mysteries. We don't know how they spawn or where exactly they spawn in the Sargasso.

When eels first reach the estuaries, they are already three years old, having been carried by the Gulf Stream to Europe from the Sargasso Sea – an incredible journey of 4,000 miles. They are completely translucent and known as 'glass eels' before they enter the river and turn a brown colour for camouflage, becoming elvers (see page 76). They have a powerful instinct to move upstream, sometimes leaving the water in damp conditions and moving over land.

Eels were once one of the most common fish species in rivers, and prior to the Industrial Revolution they made up 50 per cent of all freshwater fish catches. In recent years they've suffered a catastrophic decline, becoming critically endangered. There's a litany of reasons for this decline, including barriers to migration, climate change, parasites and overfishing. The black market for elvers is now worth £2.5 billion per year as the demand for them grows in Asian markets.

MARSH SAMPHIRE *Salicornia europaea*

A specialist of coastal and estuarine environments, marsh samphire grows on salt marshes and beaches, sometimes forming big, green, fleshy carpets. As a succulent, it has a high water content, which accounts for its slightly translucent look. This is one reason for its descriptive name 'glasswort', the other being the traditional practice of burning it to create soda ash for use in glass making.

It's commonly used as a side dish with seafood, having a spinach-like taste and texture and a natural saltiness. It has other names such as 'sea asparagus' and 'picklewort'. It is low in calories and high in vitamins and minerals, particularly vitamin C, calcium and magnesium.

Marsh samphire has specialist adaptations that allow it to thrive in saline environments, including salt-excreting glands that help manage salt levels. Because it grows well in muddy and salty environments, it helps stabilise the banks of the estuary, preventing them from being washed away into the sea.

GREY SEAL *Halichoerus grypus*

Although they are marine animals, grey seals will push up rivers to find food, and the estuaries are a favoured hangout as they often have plenty of fish to eat. The British Isles are home to 40 per cent of the world's grey seal population, with the majority of those on the Scottish coastline. One of the larger breeding colonies is at Donna Nook in Lincolnshire (see page 79), due to its sheltered location on the Wash estuary and the availability of food.

Grey seals have grey and brown fur, sometimes with a pattern of blotches. They lack visible ears, and have a long muzzle with parallel nostrils. A little bit unfairly, their scientific name means 'hook-nosed sea pig'. Grey seals are larger and darker than the harbour seal. The males can exceed 180kg in weight while the female is closer to 135kg. They have a layer of blubber around 10cm thick to keep warm in the cold seas.

Female grey seals live longer than the males – up 35 years – while males can live to around 25 years. When born, grey seals are covered in white fur which isn't yet waterproof, so they stay on the beach until they shed this a few weeks later. It's thought that the white fur is a legacy from when these seals lived in colder climates.

THE ESTUARY

OYSTERCATCHER *Haematopus ostralegus*

Despite the name, oystercatchers don't exclusively hunt oysters but have a wide diet of worms, molluscs and crustaceans. This varied diet means that different oystercatchers can specialise in particular prey and this, in turn, affects the bill shape. You have the stabbers, chisellers and hammerers – and the same individual may switch from one specialism to another depending on prey availability.

With all this wear and tear, you'd think the oystercatcher would find easier prey, but the bill of an oystercatcher grows at an astonishing rate, up to 0.4mm a day. The eyes, like the bill, are red, while the plumage is black on top and white on the belly, with dark pink legs and feet.

A group of oystercatchers is called a stew, and they are often found in groups. They are feisty birds and will attack would-be predators in groups when they feel threatened. The call is a sharp whistle-like blow and a staple of any estuary soundscape.

Over the last half-century, more and more oystercatchers have been breeding inland near large gravel pits, fishing lakes and even on top of tall buildings in city centres. Oystercatchers often travel inland in the winter to escape storms and find food, and if they find ideal breeding conditions, will stay put rather than returning to the coast.

EEL GRASS *Zostera spp.*

Eel grass is unusual as it's one of the few flowering perennial plants that grows in the subtidal zone (an area close to the shore but always submerged). It is typically found on substrates of gravel, sand or sandy mud in areas where it is protected from exposure to the full force of wave and tide action. This often means estuaries are the perfect habitat for this important plant. Eel grass acts as a vital nursery for juvenile marine fish and a home for protected species such as seahorses.

It lives on the very low shore up to 10m deep, and can form dense seagrass meadows. It gets its name from its long, eel-like leaves. Not having insects to pollinate the flowers, eel grass plants simply release long, thread-like pollen that drifts in the tide, becoming entangled in the grappling-hook-shaped female stigmas of other eel grass plants. The plants also have a rhizome, a type of underground root system that allows new plants to grow vegetatively.

Eel grass is susceptible to physical damage from activities such as boat mooring, bait digging and dredging, which it can struggle to recover from if not given a chance. In the UK, half of the seagrass meadows have been lost since 1985. To help tackle this, many groups have started to harvest seeds and replant them in suitable areas to help meadows recover.

FLOUNDER *Platichthys flesus*

This flatfish has a rather unique skill among marine fish, in that it can travel well into fresh water and even stay there for months. Flounder breed in the sea but the young will head to estuaries for shelter and food. Some take this to the next level and, providing there are no barriers stopping them, will travel more than 40 miles inland.

These small flatfish often spend the summer in the warm and food-rich water before dropping back down into salt water during the winter. Like all flatfish, they are born with eyes on either side of the head, like most fish species, but as they grow the left eye migrates towards the right, on top of the head, and the downward-facing side of the body becomes pure white. This is because they are bottom-dwelling fish and hunt food by looking towards the surface. Flounder can change colour rapidly to fit in with the substrate they are lying on, and experiments in which flounder are placed on a chess board have shown that they will mimic the pattern. Although thought of as an ambush predator, they will also chase shoaling fish into mid-water to feed. Flounder typically spawn in the open water, with eggs and larvae drifting in the currents until they settle on the sea floor.

MITTEN CRAB *Eriocheir sinensis*

While many species of crabs will be found in the mixed waters of the estuary, only one species can move up into completely fresh water: the Chinese mitten crab.

This non-native species was accidentally introduced into large river systems like the Trent, Thames and Welsh Dee, likely via ballast tanks, a common transfer method for invasive species. They originate from China and East Asia and are considered a delicacy there.

Mitten crabs get the 'mitten' part of their name from the hair-like bristles on the claws. The body is about the size of your palm and the legs spread out to 12cm, making this a decent-sized crab.

In the autumn, the crabs migrate downstream to spawn in brackish water, congregating in huge numbers in the estuary. Unfortunately they do impact native species by eating pretty much anything they can grab, as well as by burrowing into riverbanks and causing them to collapse. In fact, these crabs are so aggressive that they will out-compete other non-native crustaceans like signal crayfish, which are seldom found in the same areas.

THE ESTUARY

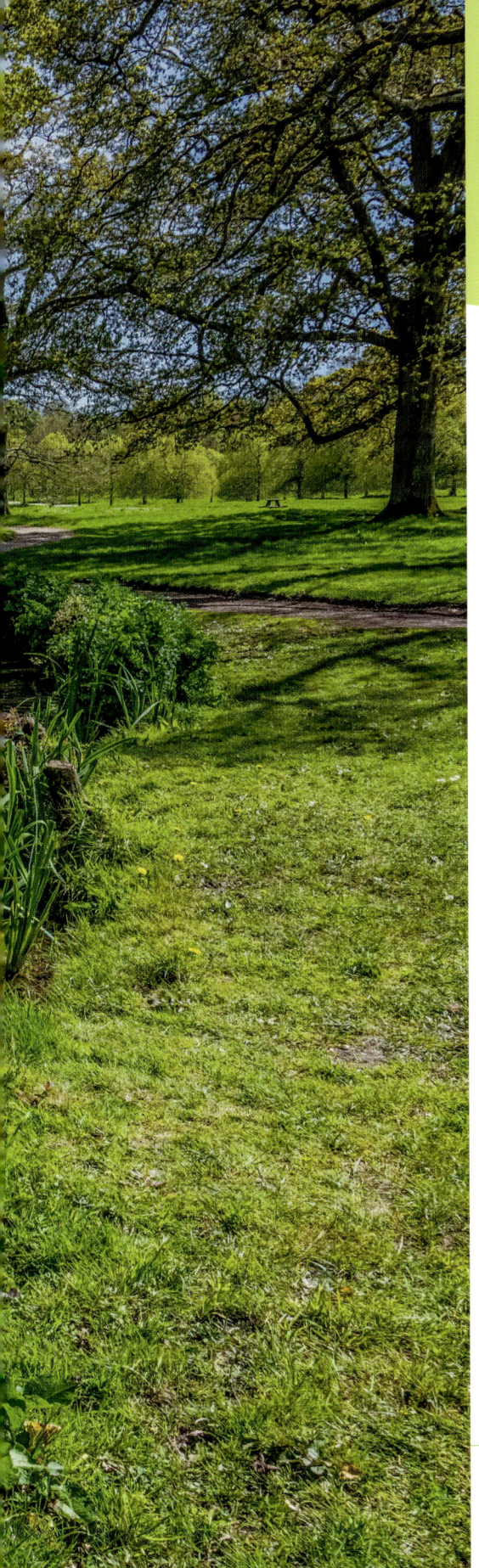

6

Chalk Streams

Here in Great Britain, we have one of the rarest habitats on earth: the chalk stream. Of the 260 chalk streams that can be found in Europe, 85 per cent are in England, with the rest in northern France. This is an internationally scarce and important habitat; many people in England aren't even aware of it, yet it's like having our own Great Barrier Reef right on our doorstep.

The lion's share of chalk streams are in southern England, with the best-known examples being the Test, Itchen and Hampshire Avon. However, they follow a large chalk band into Sussex, Kent and even south London, as well as East Anglia and up into Lincolnshire and east Yorkshire.

← In its upper reaches, the Kennet shows off the crystal clear water characteristic of chalk streams.

What is a chalk stream?

When I think of a chalk stream, I picture water so clear that it looks like the trout are floating in mid-air, with rafts of flowering water-crowfoot. Sadly, this is something of a daydream nowadays, for all the usual reasons behind river decline such as sewage and agricultural pollution, invasive species and bankside erosion.

They are typically lowland rivers with little gradient to them and, although they have pace in stretches, they typically move at a slower rate. What makes them so special is a quirk of geology: they have underwater chalk aquifers through which water is pushed, making the water at this part of its journey clean and clear. This chalk was formed 60 million years ago, deep under the sea, by the compression of microscopic plankton that had settled to the sea floor. The water makes its way up to the surface and in some places you can see it pushing from the riverbed. This unique process means that chalk streams typically stay at the same temperature all year round. Whether it's the height of summer or a bleak midwinter, they are always around the 11°C mark. The constant flow of water also means that most chalk streams remain at a similar height for most of the year, only changing in periods of extreme flooding or drought. They often have multiple channels splitting off, some of which are natural but many were dug for mills and relief channels. This has created lots of backwaters that many creatures call home.

↑ Brown Trout are a popular target for fly anglers on the River Test.

Straightening rivers

If you could travel back in time to before the Romans invaded Britain, the chalk streams, and indeed many rivers, would have been very different. To allow boat traffic, humans widened rivers like the Test, Itchen, Avon and many others. They also straightened the rivers and diverted side channels to make one single deep river. This meant the surrounding land was drained and farmable, as well as allowing boats to travel upstream.

The problem with this, which still persists on many of the premier chalk streams today, is that the rivers basically became glorified canals. What would have been myriads of islands, branching side streams, sunken willows and riverbanks fringed with woodland have been turned into deep mucky rivers with all the flow and vigour of a spilled milkshake. Don't get me wrong – these areas still hold plenty of amazing species, but they could be so much more. In recent years, efforts have been made to put bends back into rivers, to allow trees to fall in, to create gravel bars and to plant up the margins – all of these modifications are intended to help with biodiversity.

Many chalk streams were also used to create water meadows, a system of agriculture developed between the seventeenth and nineteenth centuries that shaped rivers into a patchwork of channels, sluices and hatchways. Side streams or carriers were cut off from the main channel, forming a loop around and through the surrounding meadows. Hatchways were built to control flows into and out of this network of carriers, and cuts were made across the meadows to carry water to flood the ground. The flooding was intended to protect grazing meadows from frost and to fertilise the ground with sediment.

River keepers

River keepers are not exclusively found on chalk streams, of course (if you go to Scotland, they are often called ghillies), but many of the most lucrative parts of chalk streams have some kind of guardian looking after them. In some areas, trout fishing can cost £300 a day, and if you are lucky enough to be invited to a private angling club on a chalk stream, it can cost thousands to join. The job of the river keeper is essentially to look after and maintain the river, and they are often the first to notice any issues that arise. One of the key jobs is the summer wet cut, when keepers will wade into the river with a scythe and cut some of the beds of water-crowfoot to allow patches for anglers to fish and to help a faster flow. The long-term effects of this are minimal but, of course, any reduction of habitat will have a knock-on impact. However, the keepers do generally have a positive influence on the rivers overall, and without the anglers paying money to fish these rivers, there wouldn't be any keepers to look after and maintain them. There is a balance to be struck, making sure there are areas for the anglers to fish but also ample habitat for the fish, invertebrates and other animals that use this habitat.

Abstraction

Chalk streams are not immune to the usual host of riverine threats, but one of the key threats to them is abstraction. Abstraction refers to the process of water being taken from the underground aquifers for our own use, which in some areas leaves chalk streams without enough water and, in extreme cases, they completely dry up.

In some cases, the drying up of chalk streams is a natural process, and many of these are known as winterbournes, which in the wetter colder months have plentiful water but then dry up by the summer. However in recent years, we are finding rivers have started to dry up that historically never would have. This is due to over-abstraction by

↓ River Stiffkey, Norfolk.

↑ An angler fly-fishing in the River Avon, Wiltshire.

water companies draining the aquifers and not allowing them time to recharge.

Climate change is also playing a part in preventing the aquifers from filling up. Most chalk streams are found in south-east England, which is also the most densely populated part of the country, meaning demand for water is high here. The Environment Agency has warned that within 25 years, London could run out of water, and while little of this is fed by chalk streams, it illustrates the point that water is being taken at an alarming rate.

When a chalk stream dries up, many creatures end up high and dry. Species like bullheads, river flies, mussels and many aquatic plants are the casualties. The problem is that, even if the water returns, many of these species are already lost and may take years to return, if ever.

To stock or not to stock?

Many fishing clubs add additional fish to the river, most notably brown and rainbow trout. The reason for this is that many members pay large sums of money and want to catch lots of big fish. The fish that are stocked are generally what we call 'triploid fish' (they have a third set of chromosomes that makes them sterile) and so are unable to breed with the local trout. The problem is, however, that these stocked fish are normally much bigger so they often push out the smaller, wild trout, meaning that they are forced into less productive places to feed and are more at risk of predation, resulting in declining numbers.

Stocking also creates a false economy, making the river seem like it's full of fish when there may in fact be issues that need addressing. A progressive school of thought, however, is starting to take hold on many rivers and chalk streams in England, where stocking has been stopped and the focus has shifted to improving fish habitat. This has been a remarkable success on many rivers, such as the Lathkill in Derbyshire. While not a chalk stream, it is similar in many ways, being very small and clear. In 2003, stocking was stopped here and the fishing improved, with more wild fish present than ever. The fish have been harder to catch but this makes for better anglers and encourages recovery of wild fish stocks.

Bug hunt

Rivers are superhighways for many invertebrates, and if you'd like to get a close-up view of some of them, a moth trap is a great way of doing so. Moths are mostly nocturnal, so a moth trap allows you to see and record what species are in the area despite their being difficult to see in the dark. A moth trap isn't lethal and is essentially a bright light and a box that the moths fly into and can't get out of until you release them the next day. Many types of invertebrate may also be attracted to the light, including large beetles, lacewings, caddisflies and shield bugs.

Depending on how close you are to a power source, you may need a portable power bank. Warm dry nights are the best for results, and you should avoid rain as that will break the equipment!

This survey method offers a unique view of many species you might not expect to be present on your local river, and it's something that anyone can do. Shop-bought models are available, but are quite expensive, so making your own trap can be a good alternative if you want to give moth trapping a go. The Butterfly Conservation website has a guide on how to build a basic bucket trap. You could even try a much more simple version: shine a bright light onto a white sheet at night and just wait to see what lands on it.

If you want to try and attract other insects, you could also make a pitfall trap. Just dig a small hole in the ground and place a plastic pot within it (empty yoghurt pots are perfect), then check every now and then to see if anything has fallen in.

USING A MOTH OR PITFALL TRAP

- **It's best to use moth traps in areas that are out of the way,** as if left unattended, a bright light might attract unwanted attention from people rather than moths.
- When checking the moth trap, it's best to **get up as early as possible,** as birds will quickly learn to eat any moths on the edge of the trap.
- **There are many kinds of moth traps available** to buy. I use a Skinner trap, which is fairly basic to set up. However, it can be more affordable to make your own.
- **Take good photos of the moths and insects you catch.** About 2,500 species of moths have been recorded in Great Britain, so trying to identify your catch can take some time.

- **When using pitfall traps, make sure to check them regularly** and avoid setting them in very warm or wet weather so as not to harm anything that falls in.

→ A shop-bought moth trap in a wood in Buckinghamshire.

↑ Otters are most active at night, so night time, dawn and dusk are the best times to look for them.

Night visits

How many of us have ever taken a walk along a river at night (excluding return visits from the pub)? Many river species are nocturnal, such as otters, and nighttime is the best time to spot them. One thing I've started doing in recent years is wearing a powerful head torch and walking along some of the shallow rivers to see what's coming out at night. The riverbed can be crawling with life. Crayfish are far more active at night and will clamber along the rocks, while smaller fish like stone loach and bullhead, which are normally elusive in the day, become confident under the cover of darkness. You may be lucky and even see an eel slither past.

You could get a bat detector and find out which species are hunting and roosting along the waterway, the classic waterside species being the Daubenton's bat. Each species has its own distinct frequency, and with practice you can learn to identify them. Many organisations run group bat walks, which are well worth attending.

It's a rewarding and exciting time to visit a river but of course can be dangerous, so I would recommend going out with someone else if you don't know the river well. It's also just a great experience to share with a friend.

TIPS FOR SUCCESS

- **Look for the slack water** which doesn't have as much of a ripple, as it will be easier to spot creatures there.
- **A head torch is my preferred way to search** as it frees up your hands, and many waterproof models are available.
- **If there's already a light source, like a street lamp, it's worth checking if anything is around it** that might be used to lights at night already.
- **You can adjust the beam on many torches,** so set it for the right distance to spot what's in the water. Use a low-intensity beam and avoid shining it directly at animals so they don't become distressed.
- **Make sure you wear grippy footwear,** as you don't want to slip into the river.

Where to visit

DRIFFIELD BECK, Yorkshire

Although most chalk streams are in the south of England, we do also have them further north in east Yorkshire. The Driffield Beck rises as a spring at Elmswell in the foothills of the Yorkshire Wolds. It's only a very short piece of river, around 10 miles long, and joins the River Hull at Emmotland. The beck boasts the title of most northerly chalk stream in the world, and goes by other names such as the West Beck. In winter, otters can be found along the chalk stream, and their tracks and signs are evident all over the river. In late summer, its muddy edges attract wading birds such as green sandpipers, and dragonflies may be seen scattered amongst striking stands of purple loosestrife. The wetlands at Skerne are home to marsh frogs, an introduced species normally associated with southern England. Like the chalk stream itself, these large frogs are at their northernmost limit here.

Part of the beck is a managed fly fishery, while some of it is looked after by the Yorkshire Wildlife Trust at Skerne Wetlands Nature Reserve. The Yorkshire Wildlife Trust part of the river is open to the public and has easy walking routes offering some great views. The banks of this chalk stream leach out into wet meadows, with diverse plant life such as early marsh orchid, twayblade orchid, common spotted orchid, bog bean, fleabane and a host of other plant species.

The beck is a highly prized venue for fly anglers to fish, with its good stocks of grayling and brown trout. The river even has its own fly pattern: the Driffield Dun. The art of fly fishing involves using a fake fly made from fur and feathers, often to mimic real prey items and fool the trout into taking it. Its origins are shrouded in mystery, and no one knows where it started for sure, but Driffield Beck is one of the possible birthplaces.

RIVER TEST, Hampshire

The River Test is perhaps the best known and most widely recognised chalk stream in the world (though, arguably, the Itchen could take that title too). The Test runs for 40 miles, starting in Ashe near Basingstoke, and eventually empties into Southampton Water. The name likely originates from the old Celtic word *tren*, which means 'strong' or 'force', which over time became 'Test' in English.

You can walk along parts of the river on a trail called the Test Way. It is a 44-mile-long walking route that takes you from the Test's dramatic start, high on the chalk downs, and follows much of the course down to Eling, where its tidal waters flow into the sea.

In the summer, the banks of the Test are lined with hemp-agrimony, purple loosestrife and marsh marigold and in the water itself you'll find mare's tail, water-crowfoot and starwort gently moving in the clear water. The river itself is home to many fish species, including Atlantic salmon. Recently a study found that chalk stream salmon are different from the rest of Britain's salmon, showing distinct genetic markers compared to other populations.

The Test flows through many towns, including Stockbridge, Romsey and Andover, all offering little glimpses of this wonderful river. The river has many tributaries including the Blackwater, Dun, Dever, Anton and Tanners Brook. The course and turbidity of the Test change drastically as it gets closer to Southampton; while its upper reaches are still relatively shallow and clear, it becomes much slower and murkier lower down. This increase in dirty water is due to high demands on water and the constant stream of sewage, agricultural run-off and roadside discharge entering the river from more populated areas lower down the catchment.

RIVER WINDRUSH, Cotswolds

Rising near Snowshill in Gloucestershire and running at about 40 miles, the Windrush passes through the Cotswolds and towns such as Bourton-on-the-Water and Burford. It rises at Taddington and eventually joins the Thames at Newbridge. Only a small river itself, it doesn't have many tributaries but they include the Dikler, Sherborne Brook and Slade Barn Stream.

As with many chalk streams, parts of the Windrush can look serene and beautiful while others look like a waste ground, specifically the stretches downstream of sewage outfalls. Despite it going through the town of Bourton, there are often good beds of water-crowfoot downstream, with numerous banded demoiselles flitting about. The Windrush isn't a particularly deep river and once held a good population of white-clawed crayfish before the invasive signal crayfish moved in.

Access is mixed, but there is a Windrush path between Witney and Hardwick that allows you to walk three miles along the river. The walk is pretty flat and there are plenty of bus routes and parking along it to get there. As the river goes through a few villages, it's also fairly easy to park up and walk along these stretches. Other parts of the river can be hard to access, with routes either going through private land or among high vegetation on the riverbanks.

The name 'Windrush' means 'white fen' in old Celtic, which is a reference to the abundant amount of chalk. The river gave its name to the post-war vessel the HMT *Empire Windrush*, which brought the first large group of Caribbean migrants to the UK in 1948.

CHALK STREAMS

RIVER GLAVEN, Norfolk

The Glaven runs for 10 miles in north Norfolk, rising from tiny headwaters in lower Bodham and Baconsthorpe before meeting the North Sea at Blakeney Point. The name likely comes from the old English word for 'valley', giving us a combination of 'Glean' and 'Avon' meaning 'river valley'.

Going through large estates at three different points, the Glaven has been widened to make 'on-stream' lakes with an inlet and outlet, with Bayfield Hall Lake being a prime example. This has allowed species like marsh harrier to nest in the reeds and European eels to mature in the deeper water. Flooding at Bayfield had been an issue, with a disconnected river from the floodplains and old drainage channels blocking the water. In a project headed by the Norfolk Rivers Trust, these channels were removed and a series of pools and scrapes put in alongside the river to help soak up winter floods and increase biodiversity.

Being in Norfolk, there's not much of a decline in the course, with the source only 50m above sea level. The Glaven has two major tributaries: the Stody Beck and the Thornage Beck. There are five mills along its course, which are Hempstead, Hunworth, Thornage, Letheringsett and Glandford, but only Letheringsett corn mill is currently working (the only working mill in Norfolk).

While you can't walk the entire route of the river, there are stretches at Glandford, Bayfield and Blakeney that allow close access. This small river is an excellent place to see brook lampreys spawning in the spring, making little redds over the gravel. Above the water you may spot water voles feeding on vegetation on its banks. They are still in relatively good numbers here, as are the herons, kingfishers and waterfowl found along its course. Where the Glaven enters the sea, it is an important area for grey seals which are attracted to the area for its rich feeding grounds.

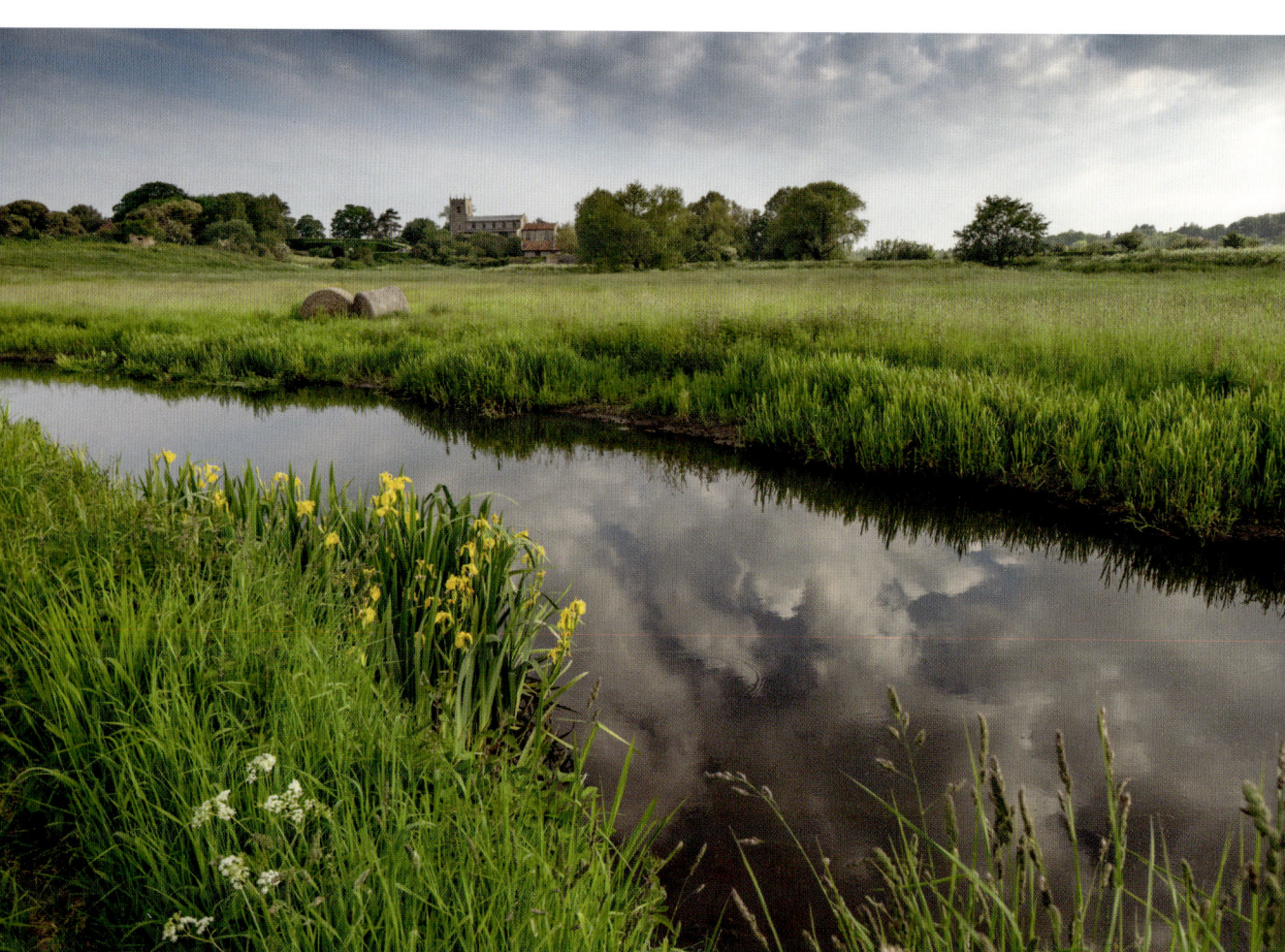

Species spotlight

MAYFLY Ephemeroptera spp.

↑ First phase adult.
← Larva.

Mayflies are among the most iconic symbols of the chalk stream, though they are found on a range of waterways. More than 50 species occur in the British Isles, but the one people most often associate the name with is the common mayfly, or green drake. It has a large body full of protein, and it's a much sought-after prey item for many riverside animals. It's a myth that mayflies only live for 24 hours, but the adult stages only last a week or so at most, and they have no mouth parts as their sole purpose is to breed.

The common mayfly typically emerges in May when the mayflower (hawthorn) is in bloom, but other species will leave the water all year round. It's the only insect to have two adult stages. First is the 'dun' stage, which is the dull, brown-coloured winged form that emerges from the water. Then, after a second moult, the duns become 'spinners', the full adult form. The larvae of mayflies thrive in silt beds, so while a river completely covered in silt is bad, having some silt beds is a positive thing for a varied habitat.

ROACH Rutilus rutilus

While salmonids are more commonly associated with chalk streams, the roach has become synonymous with their slower and deeper stretches. The water is full of food, meaning roach here can grow to huge sizes, up to 1.8kg or more in some cases, while the average roach elsewhere reaches a little over 450g. Many stretches of chalk streams that go through towns and villages harbour some huge roach looking to make a meal of any food thrown in for the ducks.

The constant temperature of chalk streams means that the roach often spawn well into May, much later than their lake counterparts. Roach spawn on plant roots in the margins, with willow roots being a particular favourite. Occasionally, they hybridise with common bream, rudd and chub.

Roach have red eyes and blood-red fins, with a silver body that has an almost blue shimmer in the light. In late summer, some roach develop a gold hue to the head, which is caused by eating lots of aquatic beetles.

Hanging around in larger shoals when younger, the bigger roach are found in far smaller numbers and are prized by many anglers.

COMMON WATER-CROWFOOT *Ranunculus aquatilis*

Aquatic plants are a vital part of any river and the clear, shallow waters of chalk streams are perfect for them. Water-crowfoot prefers moving water and provides an important habitat for small invertebrates and fish fry to hide away in, as well as providing food for waterfowl such as swans and mallards.

The stems of this plant are long, with mutliple dark green strands coming off them. The flowers are white with some yellow in the centre, looking a bit like buttercups, which are in the same family. They wriggle in the flow quite gently, and pieces that break off can take root downstream. It has several other common names including ram's foot, water buttercup and water snowcap. There are several other species in the same family, some of which are more adapted to still water, such as the three-lobed water-crowfoot.

It's a fantastic sign of a river's health when found in large numbers, as it means a river has enough clarity for light to reach it and good enough water quality for it to thrive. Sadly, it's now declining in many British rivers due to pollution.

CUCKOO *Cuculus canorus*

The cuckoo is well known for its sneaky parenting strategy. Known as an avian brood parasite, the female cuckoo searches for unsuspecting host birds of another species and lay an egg in each nest she finds. The host parents then look after the cuckoo chick. When it hatches, the cuckoo chick immediately pushes the host's own eggs or chicks out of the nest. This brutal but effective method means the adult cuckoo can lay many eggs in other nests without the responsibility of parental care. One of the cuckoo's frequent targets is the reed warbler, which often nests along the banks of rivers in thick reeds.

Adult cuckoos mimic sparrowhawks in shape and colouration, with a long tail and striped chest, though they can be told apart when in flight due to their graduated tail.

Cuckoos can eat prey most other birds would avoid such as huge, hairy caterpillars. Living near rivers brings the advantage of huge numbers of fly life coming off the water, providing food both for the parent cuckoo and its parasitic young.

Cuckoos have declined by 30 per cent since 1995 in the UK and, because they migrate to Africa in the winter, can be difficult to study and protect.

RAGGED ROBIN *Silene flos-cuculi*

This plant gains its name from its split-end pink flowers, which have a dishevelled look to them. Chalk streams are a perfect habitat for this plant of wet meadows and boggy river margins, which has been in decline. With modern farming practices draining the land, the ragged robin has quite literally been left high and dry.

A perennial, ragged robin will continue to come up each year, and spreads via seeds in the autumn. The seed pods are bell-shaped and spread by wind or animals passing by and knocking the seeds onto the ground. Its stem is very slender and it generally does not grow much higher than 30cm. It can be well hidden among other marginal plants but its spindly nature means it can weave around them to find light. It tends to be in flower from May to August, with one plant producing many flowering heads. As well as the nectar providing food for many insects, some caterpillars eat the plant itself, including those of the campion and lychnis moths.

Historically, ragged robin has had herbal uses as well, with the root containing saponins. This soap substitute can be extracted by boiling the roots in water, and used for washing clothes and hair.

SEA LAMPREY *Petromyzon marinus*

Of the three lamprey species in Britain, the sea lamprey is the largest, with some individuals reaching a metre in length. Born in the river, sea lampreys spend some time filter-feeding in the silt before heading out to sea for a diet richer in protein.

Sea lampreys are parasites, and attach themselves to large fish to feast on the blood. After a couple of years, they return to fresh water and the females create a redd, much like salmon and brook lamprey (see page 36). This typically occurs in June, when you may see several males vying for the attention of a female until one eventually wraps himself around her and spawns.

The lamprey itself is a mottled mix of yellows, browns and blacks with a circular sucker-like mouth and rows of sharp teeth.

While it's unlikely that they return to the exact river they were born in, sea lampreys are picky about where they spawn. They use their incredible sense of smell to track down young sea lampreys, called ammocetes, which encourages the adults to move upstream. If there are young lampreys present in an area, the adults know that it has previously been used for successful spawning. This method of finding suitable spawning habitat also means that once sea lampreys are lost from a catchment, they are unlikely to return on their own.

SIGNAL CRAYFISH *Pacifastacus leniusculus*

One of the most infamous invasive freshwater species is the signal crayfish. Originally from North America, it was brought over by the aquaculture sector as a bigger and quicker-growing alternative to the native white-clawed crayfish. Unfortunately, as is often the case, some escaped and the species is now found across much of Britain.

Signal crayfish have a whole rap sheet of offences, outcompeting and predating the native crayfish but also carrying a fungus colloquially called the 'crayfish plague'. Signals also burrow heavily into riverbanks, which causes them to erode, altering the flow of the river and choking gravels that fish use for spawning. It's often claimed that crayfish predate small fish but there's little evidence of this – most fish are quick enough to get out of the way.

For details on how to tell the two crayfish species apart, see page 35.

GOLDEN WEEPING WILLOW *Salix × sepulcralis*

Often found in moist clay-based soil, the golden weeping willow has inspired numerous painters and poets, featuring in many artistic works over the years. It is not a particularly large tree, growing up to 12m tall with around an 8m spread, but they more than make up for this in character, with their long, dangling branches and leaves swaying in the wind. During the autumn, the leaves turn a spectacular golden colour. It is actually not a natural species but rather a hybrid between the traditional golden willow, a native to most of Europe, and the weeping willow, which was introduced from China via traders.

Mostly found in parks and estates as an ornamental tree, it is also present in small numbers in wilder areas. The leaves tend to show from March to October and can be quite bushy, with astonishing growth rates – one of the reasons these hybrids were created was to produce shady areas quickly. The droopy nature of willows has evoked images of sadness and reflection for hundreds of years, but the real reason these willow trees are so floppy is more pragmatic – when a branch snaps off, it will fall into the river and be carried downstream where it can regrow elsewhere. This amazing regenerative ability means willow trees can essentially clone themselves to make a new tree.

MARE'S TAIL *Hippuris vulgaris*

Not to be confused with the invasive plant of the same name (*Equisetum arvense*), this species is a native aquatic plant often found in slow-flowing rivers across the British Isles. Its other common names include bottle-brush, cat tail and witch's milk. Often found in sunny areas, it thrives in open patches of water. Where the flow is moderate, it typically stays submerged and acts as an oxygenator but, if growing in the margins or low flows, it may break the surface and grow upright. In the winter, these protruding stalks will retreat back underwater to keep away from damaging frosts.

With a preference for non-acidic waters, mare's tail does very well in alkaline chalk streams and it can form dense mats, providing valuable shelter for small fish and insects. Dragonflies will often climb up the stems to emerge, and its root system can be full of small shrimps such as *Gammarus* and hoglice.

The narrow leaves grow in whorls around the stem and produce shoots to spread out, making it look like quite a primitive plant. It sometimes produces flowers, which look like a small red ring around the stem, but it can spread easily enough just by rhizomes.

BEAUTIFUL DEMOISELLE *Calopteryx virgo*

It's not hard to see why this damselfly is called the beautiful demoiselle, with males sporting a striking metallic green body and wings. The females are slightly less flashy, with brown wings. There is another closely related species called the banded demoiselle, which looks very similar, but the males have dark patches on the wings. These are the only two damselflies in Britain that have coloured wings. The flight is quite butterfly-like, with a gentle flutter to it.

Male demoiselles court females by settling on a patch of weed and then moving erratically, or 'dancing', in the air. Any intruders will be swiftly seen off, and once a female shows interest, the pair will mate. If the female has already mated with another male, the new mate will remove the previous male's sperm and deposit his own. To prevent this happening with his own sperm, he will then guard the female until she is ready to lay the eggs. The female then does something very unusual for an adult damselfly: she climbs down the stem of an aquatic plant below the surface of the water and lays up to 250 eggs.

This damselfly species is sensitive to pollution and has a mainly westerly range in Britain, with a few isolated pockets in the Lake District, western Scotland and the North Yorkshire moors. Fast water with a sandy or gravelly bottom is preferred, with the larvae hiding away in aquatic plants. The adults are on the wing for a relatively long time, from the end of April to September.

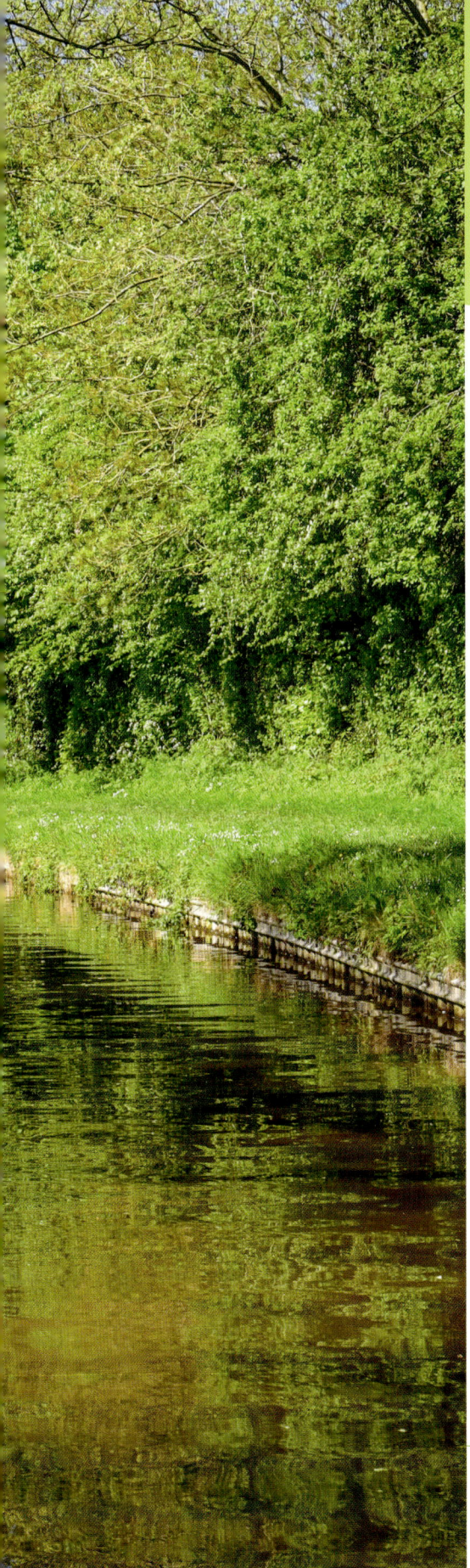

7

Canals

Canals are human-made structures that we've been using for hundreds of years to transport goods. Often connecting rivers that geographically have no natural link, canals account for thousands of miles of extra waterways across Great Britain. Birmingham, with more than 100 miles of canals, famously has more canals in it than Venice does.

For a long time canals were integral to trade and transport, with basic ditches and dykes going back to the Roman period and the first 'true canal' in England, the Bridgewater Canal, completed in 1761. This didn't last forever, though, because the growing railway network was a more efficient means of transporting goods. From 1840, the use of canals began to decline and from the beginning of the twentieth century, as the road network became progressively more important, canals became uneconomic and were abandoned. This abandonment, however, was to the benefit of many creatures, as canals started to become quieter and even, in many cases, completely left alone by humans.

← Llangollen Canal near Whitchurch, Shropshire.

These days, canals are mainly used for narrow boats and activities such as angling and paddling. Being built structures, canals can deteriorate over time, so constant maintenance is needed, which is most often provided by the Canal & River Trust, or other smaller local charities.

The water can be quite clear but generally, with the constant movement of boat traffic, it's murky and turbid. The bottom is a mixture of rock, silt and whatever else ends up sinking into the canal. To make them navigable for boats, canals are kept at a constant depth with sloping sides, the water level controlled with a series of locks that allow water into different sections and enable boats to safely reach higher or lower ground. This also means that the flow is quite slow, and so many species that prefer slower-moving water, such as ruffe, dragonflies and water voles, thrive in canals.

Some canals have been totally abandoned, such as Cromford and Grantham Canals (see pages 111 and 114), with no boat traffic passing through. Nature has quickly reclaimed these, with reedbeds and aquatic plants carpeting the shallower reaches and transforming the canal into more of a tiny strip of wetland than a highway for boats.

↓ Erewash Canal, Derbyshire.

Litter in waterways

As most canals, like many rivers, pass through built-up areas, huge amounts of litter can be blown or thrown into the waterway, from the classic traffic cone to water bottles. Poor screening on sewage works also means many plastics end up coming from sewage outfalls, such as microplastics from laundry and health and beauty products. A Greenpeace study in 2019 surveyed 13 rivers across Great Britain for traces of plastic and all tested positive. According to the survey, the River Mersey contains proportionally more plastic than the Great Pacific Garbage Patch, one of the most plastic-polluted expanses of water in the world.

The long-term effects of plastics in our waterways can be disastrous. Over time, plastics break down into smaller and smaller pieces, which can end up in the food chain, with fish and aquatic invertebrates eating them. The quantity of plastic then builds up in predators higher up the food chain, such as herons, otters, dippers and, of course, humans. This is an issue because plastic attracts and absorbs various toxins that slowly poison the larger animals. An analysis of Environment Agency data by the Rivers Trust in 2023 found that many of the freshwater fish caught in Britain, such as trout, contain such large amounts of toxins that even eating a single portion once a month would be considered unsafe

according to the European Food Safety Authority (EFSA) standards. One of the easier ways to reduce microplastic levels is to remove large pieces of plastic before they break down, and many River Trusts and volunteer groups organise river and canal clean-up days. These groups are always looking for people wanting to make a difference, so why not look up events in your local area if you're interested in helping out?

Measures have also been taken by the UK government, banning plastic straws and other single-use plastics, as well as the introduction of a charge for carrier bags. The public's attitude toward plastic use has also started to shift, helped in part by high-profile documentaries such as the BBC's *Blue Planet 2,* which featured a piece on the subject of plastics in oceans and the devastating effects it can have on marine wildlife.

To play devil's advocate, some types of non-plastic litter can in fact be beneficial, like the humble shopping trolley thrown into a canal or river, which can provide shelter for small creatures as it becomes covered in weeds and roots. In an ideal situation, a sunken tree would be better but a perch doesn't much care. I should clarify – I'm not suggesting you start stealing trolleys from supermarkets to throw into the water! However, some litter that isn't plastic-based can have short-term benefits when no natural shelter is available.

Invasive species

As long watercourses with little to no flow, canals can be colonised by many species, which then move to other watercourses. This is great for species like water vole, which need all the help they can get, but it does mean that species we may not want can also establish a foothold.

Non-native species can be introduced in a variety of ways, sometimes hitching a lift in the ballast water of boats, or even attached to the boats themselves, as in the case of zebra mussels (see page 119). Most don't need much space or water to sneak in – the aptly named demon shrimp (see page 132) can survive in the crease of an angler's waders or inside a kayak.

Some of these species are fairly benign, and slot into our freshwater ecosystem without causing any issues; for

↑ Bloody red mysid, an invasive species found throughout Europe and the British Isles.

← Invasive plant species (giant hogweed, Japanese knotweed and Himalayan balsam) along the River Stour, Worcestershire.

example, the bitterling, which is a small fish originally from mainland Europe (see page 55). However, some species become a problem and are classed as an invasive species. A species like wels catfish, for example, a large predatory fish that can weigh more than 45kg and reach 180cm long, would be quite destructive if established in British rivers. Currently present in small numbers, they're thought to have either been accidentally introduced from fishing lakes during floods or misguidedly released into rivers by anglers. If they were to reach high numbers, they would cause massive ecological damage to the rivers' food webs.

With the huge interconnection of canals to rivers, marinas and docks, if one invasive species gets in, it can spread at an alarming rate. The rather sad truth with most freshwater invasive species is that once they are established, there's often little you can do to completely eradicate them, so prevention of their spreading to new watercourses is vital. As individuals, one of the key ways we can help with this is to follow the 'check, clean, dry' initiative (see below) whenever we take part in any water-based activities, be that fishing, diving, paddling or boating.

While this may seem a little over the top to some, many invasive species can have a huge impact, from floating pennywort clogging up waterways and stopping boat traffic to signal crayfish burrowing into riverbanks and collapsing them, affecting the flow and turbidity of the water. If we can stop species from spreading to other locations, it's worth the hassle. And there have been cases of successful eradication of non-native species. For example, the South American coypu, a large rodent, was at one point widespread in East Anglia, with more than 20,000 individuals in the wild before they were eventually eradicated in 1981. These large rodents caused agricultural damage, dug into riverbanks and outcompeted native species. Another is the black bullhead catfish, a North

CHECK, CLEAN, DRY

- Firstly, **check** anything that's been in the water: fishing gear; watersports equipment; wetsuits etc. Look for anything that stands out – any bits of water plant, aquatic animals crawling around, bits of dirt stuck on, or pools of water. This should be done on site before moving away and anything found should stay on the site you've been in.
- Then **clean**, if possible using hot water, to kill off any industrious invaders. If hot water isn't available and you enter the water a lot, it's well worth investing in a small canister of disinfectant, which you can spray over any equipment.
- Lastly, **dry** the equipment, either in full sun or somewhere undercover in the wetter months. Some invasive species can survive in damp conditions for up to two weeks, so the first two steps are important to stop something hanging on.

↑ Cycling offers a quick and green way to see long stretches of rivers in urban areas.

American species that, like the coypu, is running rampant across mainland Europe but is now no longer present in Great Britain thanks to the work of the Environment Agency.

Cycling

While many riverbanks may require a sturdier bike, the canal towpath is perfect for any cycling skillset. As cycling is a green way to travel, your carbon footprint is zero and you get some exercise as a bonus. If you are just starting, canals are fantastic places to cycle long distances as there are no hills or heavy inclines and, being footpaths, there's also no traffic.

The surface is often quite smooth so your bike and body don't take too much of a battering and you get a fantastic view of the water and the life living along it. It's key to use a little common sense and consideration when cycling. Canal towpaths can be quite narrow, being built more than 200 years ago to be just wide enough for a horse that's pulling a barge. If you see people bunched up, slow down and ring the bell, giving them plenty of notice to move out of the way. Canal towpaths

TIPS FOR TOWPATH CYCLING

- **Wear a helmet,** as towpaths are generally slabs and concrete and if the worst happens and you fall off, you want protection for your head.
- **When taking blind corners or tunnels, it's best to slow down** and give a ring of the bell to let people know you are coming.
- **Soak up the wildlife and history** of the canal. Being on a bike means you can see a lot more in a day than on foot or on a boat.
- **When cycling at night or in the evening, remember to have lights** on the bike and, if possible, a high-visibility jacket, as most towpaths are unlit.
- **A puncture repair kit is a good idea** as towpaths can have an array of sharp objects like thorns, broken glass and pins that can burst a tyre.

are not public rights of way but permissive, so this means routes can sometimes be closed for maintenance.

If you want to cover plenty of ground and take in the sights and sounds of the waterway, there's no better way to travel.

Boat rides

Probably the first thing many of us conjure up in our heads when we think of a canal is the narrow boat chugging by towards a lock. For some it's a home and a way of life and for others a weekend getaway. Regardless, it's the best way to immerse yourself in the life of a moving waterway for a prolonged period.

Most of the larger canal networks in Britain have companies that hire out boats for the day, or for longer breaks if you have the funds. You can expect to travel around 4–7 miles per day in good weather so it's important to plan a rough route out. The whole point of boating is to take your time and drink in the scenery (and maybe the odd beer unless you're the one in control of the boat!).

In general, narrow boats are fairly easy to operate. The boats tend to be fully kitted out with kitchens, showers and beds so you aren't roughing it by any stretch of the imagination.

HIRING A BOAT

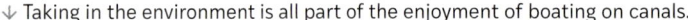

- No licence is required to drive a narrow boat, but **you need to be 18 or over.**
- It may look easy but for first-timers it's best to **take it slow and steady** and, if possible, be joined with someone who's navigated locks before so they can show you the ropes.
- **It's much like driving:** you keep to one side, usually the right, and it's important to plan your route and allow plenty of time to get to your destination before nightfall. Most routes will require you to turn back in a basin, although some are circular.
- **When mooring up, make sure you are allowed to do so** and are in a designated area. It's worth checking, as some places may charge for it.
- **When in a lock, make sure the boat is kept forward of the cill** (step) inside the lock. Check all paddles and gates are shut after you have used a lock, unless you see another boat approaching.

↓ Taking in the environment is all part of the enjoyment of boating on canals.

Where to visit

CROMFORD CANAL

The Cromford Canal runs for 14.5 miles in Derbyshire, joining Cromford with the Erewash Canal at Langley Mill. The construction of the canal was completed in 1794 and the site has a wealth of industrial heritage, lying in the Derwent Valley Mills World Heritage Site, including old railway workshops, a pump house and an aqueduct.

The canal is now largely non-navigable, which has allowed lots of reeds and aquatic plants to cover it, providing a fantastic habitat for many species, and it has become an excellent site to see water voles (see page 117). People have travelled across the country to see the voles here, with a few hotspots along High Peak Junction, Ambergate and Whatstandwell. Numbers peaked in the 2000s, but in more recent years the voles seem to have become more reclusive and harder to spot. The canal also has a healthy population of little grebes (see page 116). These small diving birds are normally quite hard to see close up but on Cromford are quite accessible. Fish numbers in the canal are fairly limited, with mostly pike and the odd brown trout washed in from the Derwent at the Cromford end. Further down, you get more perch and tench. Angling, however, is not permitted on the canal.

The towpath is very accessible, with multiple areas to park up along it and walk the sections, and there are cafés dotted along its route. There are toilets at the Cromford end but most of the canal runs through the countryside, with few facilities directly on its banks.

If you want to explore the canal by boat, you can go on the *Birdswood*, which leaves Cromford Wharf and heads towards High Peak Junction. Tours run throughout the week, and you can sit back and enjoy the views. The boat has an electric engine, but there are special trips throughout the year where it is drawn by horses for those who want to experience a more traditional style of boating.

GRAND UNION CANAL

Officially 137 miles long, the Grand Union is the largest canal in Britain, linking London to Birmingham. However, if you add up all the arms, it totals 286 miles. The canal may still yet grow, with a proposed link-up scheme from Milton Keynes to Bedford – although this has been talked about since 1810! The canal was not constructed all at once, but is instead the result of various canals being amalgamated and connected during the late eighteenth and early nineteenth centuries. This is why it's called the 'Grand Union' as it has linked all these smaller canals together. It has 250 individual locks, and travels through many major cities and towns including Milton Keynes, Leicester and Northampton. It has several tunnels, including one of the longest in the country at Blisworth, which is 2.8km long!

Being so long, the Grand Union boasts a huge array of wildlife. In the London sections, you often see cormorants resting on the locks with their wings spread to dry off. They are generally much more approachable here than in more rural settings. The many tunnels and buildings along the canal make it an ideal spot to see bats in the evening, as they flit over the water to feed on the many insects hatching off the surface of the water.

Whether you want to walk the canal in Central London to enjoy a bit of nature away from city life, or see it in its full glory in the Chilterns, there are many easy walking routes to choose from. The Loughborough route is a great one, around three miles in distance, or try the Brentford to West Drayton stretch which is about 10 miles, listening out for ring-necked parakeets screeching overhead as you pass Hanwell Lock.

LEEDS AND LIVERPOOL CANAL

Built to connect two of northern England's major cities, the Leeds and Liverpool Canal runs for 127 miles – no other canal in Britain has been established to link two cities that were further apart. It opened in 1816 after 40 years of construction and has a total of 91 locks on its route.

Starting in Leeds, the canal heads north-west through Bradford, Keighley and Skipton to its most northern point in the large village of Gargrave before coming to the end at the 'Albert Dock', part of the Liverpool Docks near the River Mersey. Along the way, it runs past several major urban areas including Blackburn, Shipley, Burnley, Wigan and Bootle.

The entire length is walkable, offering views of the Yorkshire Dales and the Pennines, as well as the chance to visit Bingley Five Rise Locks, with five locks in quick succession. The paths are mostly flat and are well used, with some short inclines.

In the more populous areas, there are all the public amenities you'd expect, including parking, toilets, cafés and one or two decent pubs! There are also many canal boat hire companies along its course, which can be a great way to explore the canal and take in the surroundings.

Grey herons line the banks of this canal, looking for an easy meal in the margins. If you explore some of the more rural routes, you have a chance of seeing brown hare, roe deer and foxes.

Like many canals, it does have its fair share of invasive species and in areas like Skipton it is infested with signal crayfish (see page 102). These non-native invaders degrade canal banks and cause thousands of pounds worth of damage. Although technically edible, the canal crayfish are often full of heavy metals and pollutants due to their detritus-eating habits, and are therefore not worth eating!

GRANTHAM CANAL

Originally 33 miles long, this canal connected Nottingham and Grantham, primarily to transport coal and other goods. I say originally, as a three-mile segment of the canal is now dry due to leaks and the stretch below Cotgrave only has one small feeder stream. During extended warm periods, it's likely to dry out. Above Kinoulton, the canal starts to retain its flow and depth a bit more. It has 18 locks, although most are now defunct and sealed to maintain a stable water level.

Although some sections are used by boats, the canal is largely untouched these days, and nature has regained control for most of its length. It's more like a continuous long pond, with dragonflies filling the air in the summer, frogs breeding in its reedy margins in the spring and migratory birds passing by in the autumn. It has plenty of plant life too, as there are few boats to stir it up, with patches of yellow waterlily, frogbit and dense beds of hornwort, an oxygenator.

The towpath is well maintained and offers numerous lovely walking routes and stop-off points such as the old wharf tearooms at Hickling and the Dirty Duck pub at Woolsthorpe. The canal passes by the towns and villages of Cotgrave, Cropwell Bishop, Harby and Bottesford, snaking its way through three different counties: Nottinghamshire, Leicestershire and Lincolnshire.

There are rumblings about trying to reopen the canal as much as possible for boating. However, this would be rather difficult as the canal had 23 of its 69 bridges flattened and reduced to small, covered concrete pipes. Like many canals in England, it's managed by the Canal & River Trust, but it also has its own dedicated group called the Grantham Canal Society, which for more than 50 years has supported and raised funds for the canal.

Species spotlight

GUDGEON *Gobio gobio*

Canals are the perfect habitat for the gudgeon, a small bottom-feeding fish that likes slow-moving water with some turbidity and plenty of hiding places, which canals have in abundance. Found in large shoals typically near the bottom, gudgeon will also come higher up the water column. They often spawn over sandy beds, which are frequently found at the lock gates in canals where the water rushes through every time a boat comes through.

Gudgeon get their name from the French 'goujon' as they were often fried and eaten whole in the past. They typically grow to around 10cm in length, although bigger specimens can reach 20cm. With a large mouth relative to their size, they engulf any small morsels that will fit into it, using their two barbels to taste the water for food. They have some beautiful markings on the flanks, with a collection of shiny blues, silvers and olive green. Due to this shiny colour, they are also sometimes called 'glass carp'.

MUTE SWAN *Cygnus olor*

One of the most common species of waterfowl in Britain, mute swans are often found on canals in search of a free handout from people. Using their long neck, they can reach the bottom of the canal and sift through the detritus to find food.

Mute swans pair up for life, and the easiest way to tell a cob (male) and a pen (female) apart is by the black bump on the head, located just before the bill starts – this is much bigger in male swans. Adult males can weigh nearly 10kg, making them one of the heaviest flying birds in Britain.

Despite their name, mute swans can be quite vocal, making an array of sounds including snorts, hisses and grumbles. However, unlike other swan species who have a more bugling call, the mute swan's is muffled. It is also more sedentary than other swans, with bonded pairs tending to stay in the same territory, which they will guard with gusto! They are found pretty much across the whole of the British Isles, only being absent from highland areas, with lakes, rivers and ponds all supporting them.

YELLOW FLAG IRIS *Iris pseudacorus*

Space is at a premium on the banks of a canal, so any plant found there needs to be tough. Yellow flag iris can survive both submerged and completely out of the water. Once it's established, its roots create a large raft and an important shelter for many smaller creatures along the canal.

It typically flowers from May to August and is an important marginal plant and source of nectar for many insects. The plant itself is toxic to many species, so few mammals eat it. As well as producing seeds, it can spread from rhizomes which, when detached from the main plant, are buoyant and can be washed downstream to start a new colony elsewhere in the catchment.

Yellow flag iris also plays an important part in naturally stopping erosion from boat traffic, and is often planted in busy waterways as a result. The plants create a buffer from the waves and wakes that boats make as they pass, stopping the mud from the banks being washed in.

If you look closely at its leaves, you may see some small caterpillar-like larvae. These are likely to be the iris sawfly, which munch the leaves of the iris in groups.

LITTLE GREBE *Tachybaptus ruficollis*

The little grebe is also known as the 'dabchick', derived from 'dive chick', as it is a small bird that dives a lot. These birds are often shy, but on canals with lots of people can become far more approachable – for example on Cromford Canal in Derbyshire (see page 111).

The neck is a beautiful chestnut colour, which is more vibrant in the summer, and the patch at the base of the bill has a yellow tinge. The rest of the body is a muddier shade, which can make them hard to spot against dead vegetation.

Little grebes prefer areas with dense vegetation, as their small size allows them to find prey other diving birds would struggle to access in these planted margins. Their diet is mostly small fish and invertebrates, such as caddisfly larvae, which they will grab and shake loose out of their protective shells. Another adaptation is that their legs are set very far back, which is perfect for swimming but makes it difficult to walk on land. Consequently, they rarely leave the water. Their call is a distinctive, whinnying trill.

EUROPEAN PERCH *Perca fluviatilis*

With piercing yellow eyes and tiger stripes, the perch is without doubt one of the most beautiful freshwater fish we have in Great Britain. Its tail and ventral fins are a ruby red and the scales are large with a rough texture, like sandpaper to

the touch. Most canals in Britain will have good numbers of perch, as they do well in slow-moving and murky water. They are typically found in large shoals when young, but become more solitary as they grow, perhaps hanging around in groups of four or five similar-sized fish.

A perch of 900g is a good-sized fish, but they can exceptionally weigh over 2.7kg. Perch are mid-level predators, hunting smaller fish like roach and gudgeon while being on the menu themselves for species like pike and zander. The stripes on the flanks are used for camouflage, to hide from both their predators and their prey. The dorsal fin is spiky and the gills also have spikes to protect them from being swallowed whole. Instead of sharp teeth, they have rough pads on the jaw to grip prey.

WATER VOLE *Arvicola amphibius*

Water voles were once very common along our riverbanks, but habitat loss, disturbance and the introduction of American mink has caused a 90 per cent drop in numbers since 1989. Disused canals are often a favoured habitat, being quiet places for them to dig small burrows in the banks and graze on the bankside vegetation. Early spring is often the best time to spot these little mammals as they are quite active during this period and the plants haven't yet grown too high to spot them.

Water voles are the largest vole species in Britain, weighing up to 300g. They are sometimes confused with rats, but there are a couple of easy ways to tell them apart. The water vole has a more rounded and blunt face, a shorter, hairy tail and tiny ears, whereas rats have a pointed face, a long hairless tail and large ears.

Not fussy eaters, water voles have been observed eating more than 200 species of water plant and even occasionally taking insects and small fish. Despite the name, some populations don't live by water; these are known as fossorial water voles, with the most famous examples in Britain being in the middle of Glasgow!

MARSH MARIGOLD *Caltha palustris*

This marginal plant is often found in clumps along the banks of canals. Reaching up to 50cm tall, marsh marigold has rounded crinkly leaves and yellow, buttercup-like flowers poking out in early spring. In fact, it's often one of the first plants to flower, providing nectar for many early pollinators. It doesn't like deep water – no more than 10cm – and prefers boggy and muddy areas in full sun. Once established, it will send out branches that can root and start a new plant and so, in the right conditions, it eventually carpets the water's edge. Found throughout most of lowland Britain, it's also a common garden pond plant. As a perennial, it will come up each year and is important in muddy and silty areas for stabilising the riverbanks and slowing erosion.

Another name for it is 'Kingcup', which is thought to be derived from the Old English '*cyneceoppa*', meaning 'royal head', likely referring to the plant's regal appearance, with its bright yellow flowers standing tall and proud. The green buds were traditionally marinated in salted vinegar and used as a caper substitute.

ZANDER *Sander lucioperca*

There are relatively few invasive fish in Britain, compared to plants and invertebrates, and arguably the zander might be better placed as a non-native. It was first introduced to Woburn Abbey in 1878 by the Duke of Bedford, who also had the bright idea to introduce grey squirrels, muntjac deer and wels catfish. Nearly 100 years later, it was legally introduced in the Great Ouse Relief Channel by the Great Ouse River Authority for anglers to catch. From here, largely by a few illegal introductions, the zander has spread to most of middle England and is now widespread in the canal network, with large populations in the Coventry, Grand Union and Trent and Mersey Canals.

The zander looks like a cross between a pike and perch, and is sometimes nicknamed 'pike-perch'. However, it is a member of the perch family. It has a long snout with sharp teeth, and two large dorsal fins, the first of which is spiky. The body is a silver to olive colour and, like its cousin the perch, it has banding on the flanks.

NARROW-CLAWED CRAYFISH *Pontastacus leptodactylus*

While the invasive signal crayfish (see page 102) is the most well known, there are in fact five more species of established non-native crayfish in Great Britain: narrow-clawed, spiny cheek, noble, virile and, the most outrageous-looking of the lot, the red swamp crayfish.

The narrow-clawed crayfish (also known as a Turkish crayfish) is currently restricted to a patchy network of waterways including the Regent's Canal and some larger lakes. It was first imported in the 1970s for the food trade, but the faster-growing signal crayfish eventually replaced it as the primary crayfish used for food.

This species is quite large, growing up to 30cm with, as its name suggests, long narrow claws. The overall colour is a muddy olive and they have a rough texture to the shell.

Like the white-clawed crayfish (see page 35), it is susceptible to crayfish plague, so you don't find it in the same waterways as signal crayfish, which are carriers of the plague. It does not

burrow as much as other crayfish, so the risk of it releasing sediment and collapsing riverbanks is low. However, these impressive crustaceans are predators and will eat pretty much anything they can grab so can have a detrimental impact on native species. They also breed at an alarming rate and will outcompete native crayfish.

ZEBRA MUSSEL *Dreissena polymorpha*

First found in Britain in the 1820s, zebra mussels are believed to have hitched a lift in ballast tanks coming from the Caspian Sea. They will quickly form dense mats on any hard surface they can find, including brick, rocks, boats, pipes and even other mussels, causing chaos in many waterways.

Once established, they can cause a variety of problems, carpeting the riverbed, which disrupts fish spawning and the movement of sediment to different parts of the river, blocking water pipes, and affecting watercraft when present in significant numbers. They also increase water clarity by feeding on plankton, which means that sunlight is better able to penetrate the water and stimulate the growth of invasive weeds. They filter water at an astonishing rate, with one mussel filtering one litre of water within 24 hours. When you consider there can be thousands of them in one location, this is a lot and can lead to a number of ecological issues. By filtering the water, they remove lots of important nutrients that native wildlife would otherwise feed on, and they also take in many harmful chemicals which, if they all die off at the same time, are then released back into the river, causing localised issues. It also means that species that prefer murky water are more visible and easier to predate. They smother and outcompete native mussels and are almost impossible to remove once established.

8

Urban Rivers

The classification for these is fairly self-explanatory, but I think of urban rivers being lined with graffiti under bridges, with rich carpets of shopping trollies on the riverbed, and steep banks, often with poor access. Despite the grotty nature of some of these rivers, they can also be a lifeline for many species. Cities can be a concrete desert that is inhospitable to all kinds of wildlife, so having a watercourse flow through them provides these creatures with not only a place to drink but also a relatively safe refuge, as the banks are often left to grow bushy and wild.

← River Aire, Leeds.

Around 83 per cent of the people in the UK live in urban areas, so the wildlife living in and around rivers in towns and cities become very accustomed to human presence.

These built-up rivers are often the first exposure many of us have to riverine wildlife. Whether it's a heron fishing on a sluice or a kingfisher perched on a traffic cone, that little encounter can really resonate with people. Wildlife in city centres can often be much more relaxed around people than their countryside counterparts, as they are bombarded with exposure to us humans every day. This means they are less likely to spook, and budding urban birdwatchers and photographers can get some great views.

There are also benefits for the wildlife, with cities warmer than rural areas. The City of London is on average over 5°C warmer than suburban Greater London, and the roads, pavements, and buildings will absorb heat during the day, which is then released at night. In the colder winter months, that 5° can be the difference between survival and freezing to death.

Many smaller creatures thrive, as most larger predators are reluctant to enter cities, the exception being foxes, which do quite well in many cities across Britain, including Glasgow, Bristol and London. There are also extra feeding opportunities, with people feeding ducks, for example, and the leftovers feeding the many fish species below the water and rodents above. Although bread is the duck feeder's favourite choice, it's not great for the ducks' long-term health, so bird seed, peas or corn are better options if you want to feed your local waterfowl.

→ Blackberries are often found growing along riverbanks, providing excellent foraging opportunities.

Foraging

While foraging is usually more associated with woodlands and rural areas, there's no reason why you can't get a free meal in urban areas too, and the green space around a river is often a good place to start. Perhaps the most familiar example of this is picking blackberries in late summer, when shaggy riverbanks are often full of this tasty fruit.

Clover, daisy, dandelion, pineapple weed, yarrow and plantains are all common plants that go well in a salad. As for fungi, you could potentially find any grassland species along rivers, such as giant puffballs, shaggy ink caps, and edible *Agaricus* species such as horse mushrooms or field mushrooms. It is of course critically important to be certain of your identification before foraging and preparing any of these.

One of the wonderful things about picking your own food is the freshness, so it's always best to use foraged items up quickly so they don't spoil. Alternatively, you could preserve, dry or freeze what you pick to use later, and perhaps enjoy in a tasty homemade jam or herbal tea.

As with any foraging, you should only pick small amounts and avoid uprooting an entire plant. This ensures plant populations remain healthy and leaves some for the wildlife and other foragers too. From a legal point of view, check the local by-laws, as there may be rules in place to prevent foraging, and never take anything from nature reserves or other protected areas. Never pick something if you aren't 100 per cent sure what it is, as certain plants and fungi are highly toxic if consumed and can cause illness or even death in extreme cases. It's also best to avoid picking anything growing close to the ground along popular dog-walking routes, or next to roads with heavy levels of traffic – and to wash anything before eating it.

↑ Road run-off visible in a lake.

Hidden rivers

Rivers in cities have usually been seen as a great asset for providing transport, trade, irrigation and food. However, in some cases they were deemed an awkward obstacle to be hidden. There are examples of these 'hidden' rivers in many cities but especially in London.

It's thought that 12 rivers, making up a total of 42 miles, are now buried, encased and tucked away below the streets of London, including the Fleet, the Tyburn (once rumoured to have the best salmon fishing in the city) and Hackney Brook. Some of these rivers became part of the sewage system, while others were simply just built over and forgotten. The River Effra, for example, was turned into a sewer in the 1800s and the banks of the Oval cricket ground were built using the excavated earth.

While some of these rivers do occasionally get brief glimpses of the sun, like the River Brent, they are, for the most part, largely devoid of life due to lack of sunlight and poor water quality.

Road run-off

Many roads cross over rivers, and they often have grates that allow excess rainwater to flow into the river. The trouble is that the roads often have all kinds of nasties on them that then get washed in too. A commissioned study by a Queen Mary University student identified 15 types of polycyclic aromatic hydrocarbon (PAH) pollutants, and copper being flushed into rivers from roads.

Road traffic sends about 300 toxic chemicals, for example from catalytic converters in vehicles, into rivers via drains. Microplastics, tyre wear, paint, rust, pesticides, road chemicals and garden run-off are other examples of sources of pollution washed in by the rain. There have been experiments to try to reduce this, including the installation of vortex chambers, which are large filtered drums. The dirty water goes into the device at the upstream side, the drum retains the sediment and the clean water is sent into the river.

Forever chemicals

Forever chemicals are essentially a group of synthetic chemicals called per- and polyfluoroalkyl substances (PFAS) that are persistent in the environment and can be toxic to humans and wildlife. When I say 'persistent', I mean it can take over 1,000 years for them to dissipate, and so they have a huge, long-lasting effect on the environment. The Rivers Trust recently analysed government data that shows the alarming prevalence of 'forever chemicals' in our rivers, present in fish populations at levels over 300 times the safe limits on average.

PFAS include thousands of industrial chemicals found in everyday products, from frying pans to bicycle oil and even our toiletries. While some have been banned, many others are still widely in use. If you want to limit your exposure to PFAS, filtering your tap water may reduce the risk (worryingly tap water can contain them as well). Store food and leftovers in glass containers rather than plastic ones and check labels on cookware to see if it is PFAS-free. These chemicals can be removed from rivers by using activated carbon, which soaks them up like a sponge, but this has yet to be done on a large scale.

Be a citizen scientist

For many of us, it can be incredibly frustrating to see our waterways being damaged and abused. It may seem hopeless, but there are numerous ways that you can help if you're interested. Becoming a citizen scientist is basically a fancy

↓ Heavy pollution in the River Stour, Birmingham.

→ Scoping around in the riverbed for shad eggs to find evidence of spawning.

way of saying you can collect data and information that helps inform a national study. The best example of this is probably the RSPB's Big Garden Birdwatch, in which 600,000 people take part every January, helping the RSPB to monitor how garden birds are faring.

Similarly, the Rivers Trust runs The Big River Watch each year, in which participants spend 15 minutes at their local river and record the wildlife, plants, flow speed of the water, and any signs of pollution that they see. This information helps the Trust to identify issues and build up a picture of the health of British waterways. WildFish also hosts a programme called SmartRivers, in which members of the public and groups can complete training on how to do kick samples to see what species of river flies are present in the river. As river flies are the vital building blocks of many moving waterways, this helps the organisation assess the biodiversity and water quality of our rivers.

There may be opportunities to take part in similar projects on a much more local level, so check what's going on in your area if you're interested. You can also buy water quality test kits that can be used over several months to note any declines or variations you see, or to record what animals are in the area. Even some simple home aquarium test kits will show you the levels of harmful chemicals in rivers like nitrates, nitrites and ammonia.

GETTING INVOLVED

- **Look at what projects are already running.** Many of the organisations listed on page 173 run projects and are in need of people to take part. Getting involved is a great opportunity to make a difference at a local level.
- **Home kits are generally inexpensive.** Make sure you keep notes like date, time, weather conditions, etc.
- If you do see any kind of change in a river, like outfalls expelling something they shouldn't or water leaching in off a field, **it's always worth reporting it to the relevant authorities in your area** (this will vary according to which part of the UK you are in).
- If there isn't a group already that fits your needs, why not **start one up with people in your area?**

Dog walking

Many of us like to bring our four-legged friends along for a riverside walk as it's a stimulating place for both pet and owner. if you don't have a dog of your own, why not join a friend or family member who has one or, if you know someone who is elderly or struggles to walk long distances, maybe offer to walk their dog for them. There are a few things to bear in mind when walking a dog near a river, however. One recent issue with dogs jumping in rivers,

besides the constant erosion of the riverbank, is flea treatment leaking into rivers (see also page 12). This treatment is highly toxic to river invertebrates, so much so in fact that's it's banned for agricultural use, so if you use these treatments it's best to prevent your dog from entering the water. While it's also tempting to let your dog have a drink from a river, there can be lots of hidden parasites and diseases that can make them ill, so it's best to bring a bottle of tap water and a dog bowl for them instead.

↑ Rivers are a great place to walk dogs, and keeping them on the lead helps to avoid any stress to wildlife.

THINGS TO CONSIDER

- In areas with ground-nesting birds, you should **keep dogs on leads** at all times, but especially in spring and summer. In general, dogs should always be kept under control to ensure they don't chase wildlife.
- If you want to let your dogs go for a swim, it's best to **go to a dedicated 'dog pond'**, many of which are popping up all over the country, rather than polluting a local river.
- **Always make sure you have dog poo bags!** Keep a few in your coat pockets, car doors or tie some to their lead, as it's important to pick up and bin dog poo. It can have harmful effects on both soil and water quality due to the high levels of nitrogen and phosphorus it contains, as well as potentially contaminating water with bacteria and parasites.
- **Keep a towel and spray bottle handy** so you can wash the worst of the mud off your dog (and perhaps also yourself!) before coming back into the house after a particularly wet or muddy walk.

Where to visit

RIVER WANDLE, London

The River Wandle is a chalk stream that flows through south London. A short river, it flows for nine miles from its source in Carshalton, through the London boroughs of Croydon, Sutton and Merton before joining the Thames at Wandsworth. Being a small river itself, it doesn't have many tributaries, but the Norbury Brook is one of them. Throughout the seventeenth, eighteenth and nineteenth centuries it became heavily industrialised, supporting the manufacture of textiles, paper and tobacco, with as many as 68 mills along its length.

Pretty much the whole of the Wandle is walkable, with the Wandle Trail being 12 miles long as you weave along the river's course to where it meets the Thames. It's a fantastic escape from the urban sprawl of London. Being in such an urban landscape, most of it is paved and there are plenty of places to stop for food or pop to the loo if needed. Along the trail you pass Watermeads, a National Trust site that was opened to the public in 2015 following extensive work.

The Wandle is one of the only rivers in London to support wild brown trout, as they're fairly scarce in the rest of the capital's polluted and abused rivers. Kingfishers are also a fairly common sight, and can be spotted flying up and down its course looking for minnows.

It is likely that the name 'Wandle', and that of Wandsworth, is derived from the Saxon 'Wendlesworth' meaning 'Wendle's settlement'. It also lends its name to the Wandle River in South Island, New Zealand. The Wandle has been mentioned in several books over the years, from Izaak Walton's *The Compleat Angler* to H. G. Wells's *The War of the Worlds*.

RIVER TYNE, Newcastle

Running at 73 miles long, the Tyne is well known for its many large bridges, like the Gateshead Millennium Bridge and the Tyne Bridge. It passes through various northern towns and cities such as Hexham, Wylam and, of course, Newcastle. Its source is not exactly clear as the main Tyne is fed by two rivers: the North Tyne, which rises in the Cheviot Hills near the Scottish borders and the South Tyne, which rises in the Pennines in Cumbria. It has multiple tributaries including the Rede and Tarset Burns on the North Tyne, and the Allen and Nent on the South Tyne. After both rivers join into the main Tyne, near Hexham at Warden Rock, there are a few further tributaries such as the Derwent, Ouseburn, Team and Don. The exact meaning of 'Tyne' is not known, though it's thought it could be a pre-Celtic word for river.

The River Tyne Trail is 135 miles long and encompasses both arms of the Tyne. The trail covers churches, castles, such as Featherstone Castle near Haltwhistle, and incredible landscapes, as well as offering the chance to stop off at a number of traditional pubs.

The Tyne generally has a tea-stained colour to it from the peaty soil that it flows through. It is widely regarded as the best salmon-fishing river in England due to its water quality upstream and plentiful habitat. It's one of the only rivers to stock salmon parr into the river to boost numbers.

Once the Tyne reaches Newcastle, it becomes a central part of the city. It's the location of the boat race of the North between Newcastle and Durham Universities, has a floating nightclub called the Tuxedo Princess and is home to a Sunday quayside market. The many buildings in the city centre have become home to hundreds of kittiwakes (above left), which have followed the river upstream to find perfect nesting grounds. Normally found on cliffs, they have found that Newcastle's tall buildings are an ideal substitute, and you can see them all along the quayside in the spring.

RIVER TAFF, Cardiff

Best known as the river going through Cardiff, the Taff starts as a couple of smaller streams called the Taf Fechan (Little Taff) and the Taf Fawr (Great Taff), which join up just above Merthyr Tydfil. Its main tributaries include the River Cynon, River Rhondda, Taf Bargoed and Nant Clydach. It flows through Pontypridd and on to Taff's Well, the site of Wales' only thermal spring. By the time it reaches Cardiff, it is nearly at the end of its course as it empties into the Severn Estuary.

At around 42 miles long, it's not a particularly long river but it has had a huge impact on Mid Wales as an important transport route and port, as well as being popular for leisure activities like kayaking, sea trout fishing and birdwatching.

The Taff is a powerful river, which used to fuel its many mills but also caused frequent flooding to Cardiff. To help alleviate the flooding, channels were dug to divert some of the water heading into the city. This diversion helped the construction of Cardiff train station. The river now flows next to Cardiff Arms Park and the Millennium Stadium, which is used by the Welsh national rugby team and as well as hosting other events.

There are various walking trails on the Taff, with a popular one being the Taff Trail, which runs for 55 miles between Cardiff and Brecon along a mixture of riverside paths, railway paths and forest roads.

Chub, grayling and salmon call the Taff home, and it's popular with coarse anglers. Fishing is free in most of the city. Grey wagtails, dippers and even otters can be seen along its banks. The fringes of the river are lined with many species of plant, although unfortunately non-native species dominate, including giant hogweed, Japanese knotweed and Himalayan balsam.

RIVER DON, Sheffield

The Don once held the title of the most polluted river in Europe (though that title might be awarded to another UK river soon, at the rate we are going!). From the Industrial Revolution it was little more than a dumping ground for chemicals from factories, sewage and rubbish before efforts were made to clean it up in the early twentieth century.

This river is about 70 miles long, starting in the Pennine Range west of Dunford Bridge. It is best known for flowing through Sheffield and Doncaster (the river being the city's namesake) before emptying into the Ouse at Goole. It also passes through Rotherham, Thorne and Fishlake, as well as various other towns and villages. The Don's major tributaries are the Loxley, Rivelin, Sheaf, Rother and Dearne. The probable origin of the name is the Brittonic *Dānā*, meaning 'water' or 'river'.

The river has many walking routes you can enjoy along its banks, including the Five Weirs Walk along the Sheffield to Rotherham stretch.

The banks of the Don in Sheffield are home to a range of wildlife, from dippers perched on shopping trollies or using the overhangs of bridges to sand martins nesting in brick walls. Even kingfishers have been seen using old pipes to nest in. It wonderfully mixes the urban and wild. Grayling were reintroduced to the river after heavy pollution incidents wiped out the population, and they're now thriving again. It has many wet margins, with a mixture of flowering plants attracting many butterflies such as white-letter hairstreak, small copper, meadow brown, common blue, gatekeeper and ringlet.

Unusually, fig trees grow on a stretch of the riverbank in Sheffield. The seeds do not normally germinate in the English climate, but the use of river water for quenching hot metal in some of the foundries that used to operate along its banks resulted in water temperatures rising above 20°C. At these temperatures, germination occurred. Most of the trees are more than 50 years old, and the demise of such industry along the river has reduced water temperatures, so there is no evidence of new trees growing. In the past, there were even match fishing reports of anglers catching some tropical species that temporarily lived in these warm-water stretches but their populations were often short-lived due to predators like pike, cormorants and herons.

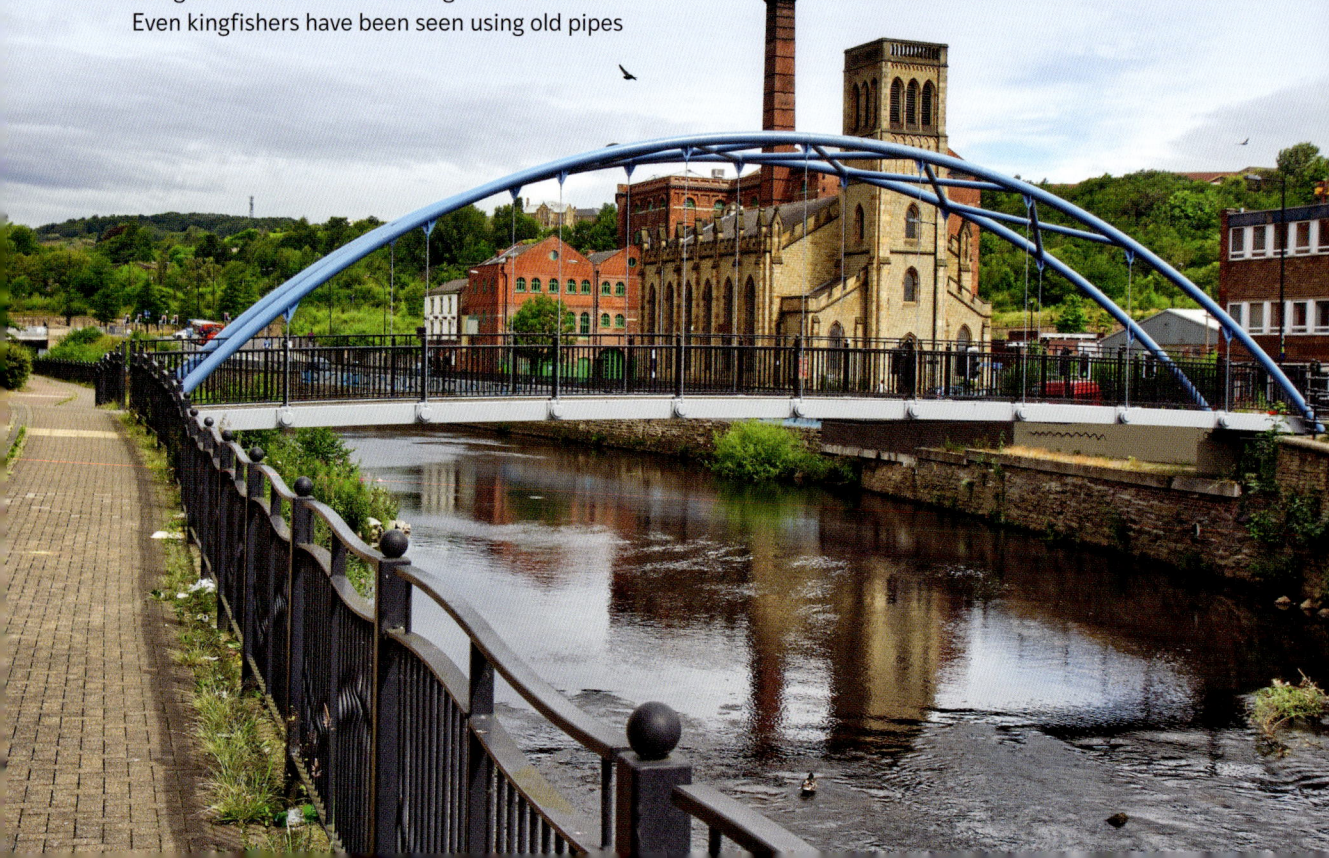

Species spotlight

BROWN RAT *Rattus norvegicus*

While not the most loved of wildlife, brown rats are often found on riverbanks. They are not native to Britain, and it's thought that they made their way to Europe in the eighteenth century via trade ships from Asia.

Brown rats will eat pretty much anything from plants and nuts to human leftovers and carrion. Many larger predators will feed on rats, such as foxes and owls, and even pike have been found with rats inside them.

Often living in loose colonies underground, brown rats can breed quickly, with females ready to breed at 3–4 months old. If food is readily available, they may breed continuously, but typically have five litters a year. Litter size usually ranges from around six in young females weighing 150g to 11 in females of 500g, but the maximum recorded is 22.

One of the concerns with rats in waterways is the spread of Weil's disease, which the rats release in their urine. Most people have mild flu-like symptoms, but the disease can be very serious. However, it's fairly rare in Britain and only transmitted via cuts or orifices coming into contact with contaminated water.

KINGFISHER *Alcedo atthis*

You may think it's strange that I've placed the kingfisher, perhaps the most iconic river species in Britain, in the urban section of the book. In truth, it could be seen in almost any area of any river.

These small, bright blue and orange birds offer a flash of the exotic when whizzing past. They are not rare by any means, but are certainly shy and secretive, so early morning is often the best time to see them. In built-up areas, the usual muddy clay banks they like to nest in may not be available so they often make do with holes in walls and pipes.

You can tell the male and female apart as males have a completely black bill while the females have orange on the underside of the bill (or if it's easier to remember, she's wearing lipstick!).

Despite their small size, kingfishers can eat quite a lot. During the colder months, they need to pack on the weight to stay warm, requiring around 15 small fish a day to survive. Spotting one can be hard but you'll often hear its characteristic whistle first, which will give you a moment to mobilise before it passes by.

GAMMARID SHRIMPS *Gammarus* spp. and others

The reason I've lumped this collection of species into a group rather than describing any particular species is that many of the shrimp species we have in Britain are very hard to tell apart from each other and don't have common names.

These little crustaceans are an important part of the food chain for many other species, and incredibly hardy. They're often the only common invertebrates present in polluted and dirty water (and therefore urban rivers), so a high abundance of them and nothing else is often a sign of poor water quality.

Although they can survive in pretty poor quality water, they aren't immune to health issues, and one species of parasitic worm (*Polymorphus paradoxus*) actively searches these shrimps out and does two things. First, it enters the shrimp

↑ Demon shrimp.

and creates a bright orange spot in the abdomen, which is normally translucent, to make it easier for predators to spot. Then, it alters the brain chemistry of the shrimp, causing it to swim around in circles at the surface where a bird might see it and eat it. The worm then breeds inside the bird's gut and the eggs are deposited back into the water where the process repeats.

Although we have many native shrimp species, some invasive ones have entered Britain in recent years, via ship ballast tanks from the Caspian Sea, including the aptly named demon and killer shrimps. These species are bigger and more aggressive than our native shrimp, and can drastically change the invertebrate numbers in rivers and lakes.

CHUB *Squalius cephalus*

These bulky fish have an incredibly greedy nature, and their name is actually the origin for the word 'chubby'. They are hardy and often do well in urban rivers even if there is pressure from pollution.

Large scales cover the fish, with a bronze colour on the flanks. It has a large rubbery-looking mouth with no visible teeth, but further back in the throat it has a set of pharyngeal teeth that are used for crushing up prey. They typically grow to around 1.4kg but can reach weights of 4kg. These fish like to hang around in shoals with similar-sized fish, with bigger chub often found with barbel.

Chub like cover, so are often seen lurking under overhanging trees such as willows, or near deep pools and bridges. They often hang around waterside cafés and pubs looking for an easy meal when people feed the ducks.

Not fussy in diet, chub will snack on anything that comes along, including slugs, small fish and, a seasonal favourite, blackberries, which is why you sometimes see them waiting under overhanging bramble bushes.

THREE-SPINED STICKLEBACK *Gasterosteus aculeatus*

This stickleback is another species that's tolerant of poor water quality and therefore found in urban areas. I remember seeing the River Stour in the West Midlands running blue from the amount of detergent in it and it still had sticklebacks in it – albeit not very happy ones!

No bigger than your little finger, these plucky little fish are found all across the British Isles from rock pools to upland streams. For most of the year they are a mottled green and silver colour, but in the spring the males develop a vibrant red pattern and bright blue eyes to attract a mate.

The male stickleback courts the female with an array of spectacular dance moves, zigzagging around to impress her. If this isn't enough, he also makes the nest for the eggs to be laid in and, after the female lays the eggs, he takes care of them. He'll clean the nest, waft it with oxygen and protect it from predators. Sticklebacks have scutes along the body, which are a larger, armour-like form of scales.

MALLARD *Anas platyrhynchos*

Mallards are quite possibly the most widespread and common waterside birds in Britain. As the mallard are so abundant, many will take it for granted, but during the spring the male sports a fine mix of vibrant colours. The head is bright green with a chestnut-coloured front and a mix of greys, browns and white on the back. The female is far more discreet, with a primarily mottled brown colour, which helps her to hide from predators when laying eggs. Both sexes have an iridescent blue wing-bar. Perhaps one of the most striking things about mallards are their orange feet, which typically go unnoticed when swimming in the water.

Adapting well to many waterways, mallards do especially well in towns and cities, growing fat on the free offerings they are fed by people. It's always worth checking flocks for other, rarer species of ducks that sometimes get mixed in, such as wigeon, garganey and teal. However, you are more likely to find dumped domestic ducks among them – these too are mallards but come in various shapes, sizes and colours.

RAMSHORN SNAIL *Planorbarius corneus*

Out of more than 50 species of freshwater snail in the British Isles, the ramshorn snail is perhaps the most striking. Its curly shell earns it its name, looking like the horn of a ram. The shell typically doesn't get much bigger than 2cm. Like many freshwater snails, ramshorns are fairly tolerant of poor water quality so, along with species like great pond snail and wandering pond snail, often do well in urbanised rivers.

The ramshorn has a red tint to its skin and shell because it has haemoglobin in its blood, much like us, while other snails tend to have haemocyanin, giving their blood a green colour. They can be prolific breeders and, being hermaphroditic, any two ramshorns can breed with each other. The eggs are laid on a hard surface and will hatch a few days later.

Feeding on aquatic plants, these small snails have an important role in breaking down material in the water. The nitrates from the snails' poo then goes on to feed the aquatic plants that they themselves feed on.

HIMALAYAN BALSAM *Impatiens glandulifera*

Of the many invasive plants along urban areas, Himalayan balsam is one of the most common, and is a difficult species to eradicate. Brought over to Britain from the Himalayas in 1839, it was a popular plant in gardens for its fast-growing nature and its attractive pink flowers.

Balsam prefers wet and shady ground, which means riverbank margins are perfect for this plant. The issue is that because it grows and spreads so relentlessly, it crowds out native plants and blocks the sunlight from reaching them. It's also very shallow rooted, which means it erodes and degrades the soil and in times of heavy rain or flood, this can cause riverbanks to collapse.

The plant has a long thin stem, skinny green leaves and large, pink flowers shaped like a bonnet. Its only saving grace is that it produces a lot of nectar and bees seem to love it. Each plant can have up to 800 seeds, which have a rather novel way of spreading. When an animal or person passes by, the vibration triggers the pods to explode, projecting seeds as far as 7m.

Removing it is difficult but not impossible, and involves finding the highest population upstream and starting there before moving downstream. Work parties carry out 'balsam bashing', as with its shallow roots it is easy to simply pick out. However, this should be done before the seeds are ready or you'll just be spreading more seeds, so before June is best.

YELLOW WATERLILY *Nuphar lutea*

This lily likes to be in the slower-moving areas of rivers, often in back channels, eddies and margins out of the faster flow. Although some of its pads rise to the surface like a traditional waterlily, many will remain submerged and look like some kind of aquatic cabbage. The pads are bright green, oval in shape and rubbery to the touch. The yellow flower is rounded, looking a bit like a Brussels sprout. It flowers from June to September and once it's finished will begin to rot, producing a sweet alcohol scent, earning it its other name, the 'brandy bottle'.

The lily has thick rhizomes, which attach to the riverbed via its roots and, if broken off, will start a new plant. Although it can live in quite turbid water, it doesn't like to be too deep and is generally found in water less than 3m deep. It is often found in dense mats on the riverbed, which creates a vital hiding space for many small fish and invertebrates to escape predators and get out of heavy flows during floods.

GRASS SNAKE *Natrix helvetica*

Although called a grass snake, this species is actually more often found by water and is an accomplished swimmer, able to dive for up to 30 minutes. The body is olive green with black vertical bars and a yellow collar. The pupils are rounded, unlike in the adder, which has vertical pupils. It's the only native snake in Great Britain to lay eggs, finding rotten vegetation on which to lay a clutch of up to 100 but more often in the region of 30.

Unlike most reptiles in Britain, the grass snake is somewhat nomadic and will travel along riverbanks to find new habitats and feeding grounds. This sometimes leads to it being found in gardens, allotments and public parks. Compost heaps and garden waste dumped by rivers in these areas are favoured for egg-laying. It hibernates in the winter, finding cover underground or in log-piles, emerging the following spring.

The main food sources for this snake tends to be amphibians, fish and small rodents, but it will also eat small birds if given the chance. It is a long-lived snake, and some wild specimens have reached 28 years.

9

Scottish Spate Rivers

While spate rivers are not unique to Scotland, it certainly has the highest concentration of them in Britain, due to the more rugged and hilly landscape and higher amounts of rain. When a river is in spate, it has more water than it normally would and is running quite fast, so a spate river is one that generally has fast flows and is prone to rising rapidly. However, unlike slower rivers, which can take multiple days to lose the excess water, spate rivers tend to lose the extra water quickly. These rivers are characterised by lots of clean rocks and boulders, with low numbers of aquatic plants. They can vary from being as clear as glass to a strong peat colour from the surrounding moorlands.

← River Snizort, Isle of Skye.

These rivers are harsh environments for their inhabitants, as they're colder and less biodiverse than rivers in the lowlands, but what they lack in species numbers they make up for in some incredibly specialised creatures. For example, larvae of flat-headed mayflies (see page 151) are horizontally compressed, allowing them to stay in one position as the flow moves over them, aided by sharp hooks on each foot to help them hang onto rocks.

Spate rivers often have high numbers of river fly species, which feed dippers and salmon parr. Larger fish like brown trout and salmon can cope with the faster flows, but their young, along with smaller fish species, have to find shelter, making use of the side channels and eddies and hiding behind large rocks and trees to escape the faster current and avoid being washed downstream. Because of the fast flows, the gravels are generally pretty clean, which is ideal for salmonids to spawn in.

↓ The River Findhorn at Strathdearn.

Floods

With the raw power of these rivers, floods can happen very quickly and as all the water gets funnelled through gorges and narrow channels, the results can be disastrous. Flash flooding happens when rain falls so fast that the underlying ground cannot drain it away fast enough. This is normally after a period of very dry weather when the ground has hardened, or in areas with lots of hard ground made of rock, concrete or stone.

So how do we avoid severe flooding? Well, it's something a lot of people have been trying to figure out for a long time. Historically, there would have been flood plains to help soak up the extra rain and distribute it over a larger area. However, over the millennia we've drained these for agriculture and housing, meaning the same amount of water that falls is passing through a smaller area and spilling out.

In many areas, the approach is to try to hold water back, for example, ensuring there's plenty of sphagnum moss in the upland reaches of the rivers to act like a giant sponge (see page 11). Further downstream, adding channels of the

→ Flooding on the River Trent.

↓ Wood in rivers provides great hiding places for young fish and invertebrates.

river to wetlands can help divert the huge amounts of water flowing down.

The comeback of the beaver (see page 53) could well help too, as – contrary to popular belief – they slow flooding rather than cause it. Recent reintroductions in the UK have been shown to alleviate downstream flood risk. Studies carried out by University of Exeter hydrologists discovered that beaver dams can increase water storage on the floodplain and slow down river flow, thereby reducing peak discharge during heavy rainfall events by 30 per cent on average.

Woody debris

For generations we've had the compulsion to remove sunken and fallen trees from rivers to keep things looking 'tidy'. However, these trees are vital to the ecosystem of many rivers, especially the fast-flowing ones.

For a start, they act as a buffer to the flow, creating creases and pockets of slower water, which provide a safe haven for many smaller creatures. Some trees remain alive and will create thick mats of roots, which are perfect for aquatic invertebrates to hide away in and, in turn, feed many small and juvenile fish. These fish also find shelter here from predators, so these woody areas are a real lifeline for small fish species. The flow around the trees also scours the gravel clean, making it a good place for salmon, trout and lamprey to spawn, while also giving them cover to duck into should a predator come by.

The fast flow of spate rivers can cause bank erosion, so large trees that have fallen in the water help to create a buffer between the fast water and the soft marginal edges, preventing the riverbank from crumbling away. The sunken trees even help the overall temperature of the river as they create shade, cooling the river down, and help to hold back the flow, both of which are crucial in periods of drought.

Waterfalls

We have more than 90 major waterfalls in Great Britain, the tallest being Eas an t Strutha Ghil in the Scottish Highlands at a staggering 290m!

Waterfalls form when rivers flow over different layers of rock with varying levels of resistance to erosion. The soft rock layer erodes more quickly than the solid rock layer, causing the solid rock

← Fairy Pools at Glen Brittle, Skye.

↓ Salmon cages off the west coast of Scotland.

layer to hang over the channel. Over time, the solid rock layer collapses, creating the waterfall. Technically speaking, any natural bit of water crashing over rocks that are higher than 150cm is officially a waterfall, but many of these may not look as spectacular as their larger cousins!

Depending on the gradient of the waterfall, it can be a valuable habitat for many creatures. Where there is a gap between the water and rock, walls are often covered in moss, and offer a safe haven for moisture-loving invertebrates. Some birds such as dippers and grey wagtails will even nest in the gaps behind waterfalls as they provide a refuge from predators like stoats and foxes.

Waterfalls with tiers and pools in them may even be passable for migratory fish such as salmon, lampreys and eels, which will move up the waterfall in stages and rest for a while in each pool. In low flows, they may well get stuck in these pools until the rain comes to help them move on.

Salmon farming

Perhaps the most iconic river species in Scotland, salmon are sadly facing a multitude of issues. Over the past two decades, numbers of wild salmon in Scotland's rivers have declined by 70 per cent.

One huge hurdle is the explosion in the number of salmon farms around the Scottish coastline.

Some open-net salmon farms put wild salmon and sea trout at risk from parasites (notably sea lice) and diseases. Farmed fish that escape threaten the genetic integrity of wild salmon and further compromise their future survival. The conditions these farmed salmon have to endure can be grotesque, resulting in the fish losing skin. The chemicals used to treat the salmon for sea lice leak into the sea, affecting marine life, as do the large amounts of fish waste polluting the seas near the nets.

One hidden issue is the use of so called 'cleaner fish'; wrasse and lumpsuckers that are harvested from the wild and put into pens to eat the lice. These fish are forced into a crowded environment, and after one season are destroyed, which is such a waste given that wrasse can live for up to 30 years. The answer is simple: don't buy farmed salmon! There are plenty of more sustainable options that you can buy instead.

Leaping salmon

One of the best autumnal wildlife spectacles is Atlantic salmon leaping up a river. Their scientific name *Salmo salar* means 'salmon leaper'. For the salmon, it's a vital part of its life cycle to reach its breeding ground.

Atlantic salmon have been recorded leaping as much as a whopping 4m in the air to clear an obstacle, but if you want to see them doing this, timing is key. You need some rain to get the fish moving and to add height to the river. Too little and they won't bother jumping; too much and they won't need to jump and can simply swim over the barrier.

If you are photographing salmon, I find it is best to use a long lens and manually focus on the area where they are jumping the most. Using a continuous shooting mode offers you the best chance to get a decent shot.

> **BEST SPOTS TO SEE SALMON LEAPING**
>
> - **Falls of Shin,** Sutherland
> - **Buchanty Spout,** Perth
> - **Rogie Falls,** Inverness
> - **Hexham Weir,** Northumberland
> - **Gilfach Nature Reserve,** Powys
> - **Shrewsbury Weir,** Shrewsbury
> - **Castle Drogo Weir,** Devon

Snorkelling

Had I written this book a decade or so ago, I'd be far more enthusiastic about snorkelling in a river but, for many reasons outlined in earlier chapters, it's something I'm a little cautious of now, although spate rivers are often cleaner than many others. I've never really considered myself a wild swimmer but I suppose in many ways I am, and I did it before it was trendy!

Snorkelling in a river is a bit like birdwatching below the water. You get to see an environment that few others do in detail. If you scan the riverbed, you can spot the many invertebrates crawling over the rocks, and if you move slowly, shoals of fish will appear.

I prefer to wear a wetsuit as it's flexible and ideal for most situations, though a drysuit is warmer for winter dips. I try to avoid swallowing water and don't go in if I have any cuts, to avoid infection.

As with many riverside activities that involve getting in the water, access is sometimes a grey area although it's generally easier in Scotland

↓ Atlantic salmon trying to jump over a weir on the River Dulnain.

thanks to the right to roam. It's best to search online for established river swimming spots to avoid conflict with other water users or accidentally trespassing, and to make sure you're swimming in a safe area. Safety is always key and if visiting a new area for the first time, it's best to go with a friend. If the water is clear, there's nothing better than a summer swim with the sun on your back and head below the water, seeing the ranunculus sway and minnows dart around.

STAYING SAFE

- **Time of year and budget will determine what you wear:** a drysuit, a wetsuit or, if you're feeling brave, just swimwear!
- **You'll have a much easier time if you wear fins,** especially when swimming against the current.
- For beginners, it's tempting to go for a full-face snorkel mask, but these have so many issues like carbon dioxide build-up, shallow breathing and difficulty clearing water from them, so **it's best to stick to a traditional mask.**
- **Stick to rivers with clear water** and avoid structures like weirs, which could take you under. If the water looks quite fast, find a slower part of the river to start your snorkel.
- **Check online to make sure there haven't been any recent sewage releases** that would make the river unsafe to swim in.

Footprint trap

Mammals can be notoriously difficult to find on our rivers, but there's a very easy and fun way to see who's around. You can either find a sandy bank or bring some sand of your own and place it down along the side of the river. Make sure it's smoothed out and then place something to cover it from the elements, like a large plant pot or cardboard box placed sideways to stop the rain hitting it but still allow the animals in. You could also just do this under a bridge or large tree, which will help protect the sand. Leave it for a couple of nights and then go and see what footprints have been left behind.

The sand should leave a pretty accurate impression of the passersby. Species such as otter, water shrew, water vole and badger all use riverbanks to move along, so you never know what may come by. You can get good footprint ID sheets online to help you tell the prints apart and it's a good idea to learn cat and dog prints as they also often end up on the sand.

If you want to take this one step further, you could also put a trail camera up to record the wildlife (see page 60), though if the area is along a busy footpath there's a risk of it being stolen. However, few people are going to nick your sand!

TIPS FOR SUCCESS

- **Find a spot that's secluded** so people don't walk through your trap.
- **Take a camera with you** to photograph the prints to help you work out what species left them later.
- **Avoid wind or heavy rain** as this will mess up the sand trap. In the winter, snow could well be used and is a great way of doing some nature detective work.
- Any species records are always gladly accepted by most wildlife groups, especially if it's something unusual, so do **share your findings online.**

↑ Otter tracks by the River Whiteadder, Scottish Borders.

Where to visit

RIVER TAY

At 120 miles in length, the Tay holds the title for the longest river in Scotland and at its widest point, it can hold more water than the Thames and Severn rivers combined.

It starts on the slopes of Ben Lui, not too far away from Oban, at a whopping 720m above sea level and joins the North Sea at Dundee. It has a few tributaries including the Earn, Isla, River Tummel, Almond and Lyon. 'Tay' comes from an extinct version of the Celtic language and is thought to mean 'strong one'.

The Tay crosses through many well-known places including Dunkeld, Aberfeldy and Perth, the latter experiencing extensive damage in 1814 when the water rose 7m above its normal height – the highest flood recorded on the Tay. One of its tributaries, the Tummel, passes through Pitlochry, where the construction of a huge dam in 1949 caused problems for salmon trying to get above it to reach their breeding ground. To solve this, a fish pass was installed to help the salmon move up the dam in stages (see page 44).

One species that does like a dam, albeit made from sticks and mud, is the European beaver, which is now found on the Tay. Trial releases in the 2000s have been successful and beavers are now fairly widespread on the river, and have even been spotted in cities like Perth.

With good numbers of small fish, you can see fish-eating birds like goosanders, red-breasted mergansers and cormorants fishing in some of the deeper pools. The Tay is also a bit of a record breaker as the location of the British record salmon. The fish was caught by by Georgina Ballantine in 1922 and weighed 29kg

With the right to roam allowing public access to most land and inland water, walking along rivers in Scotland is much easier than the rest of Britain and there are plenty of trails along the Tay, from town walks in Dunkeld to rambles on Loch Tay.

RIVER SPEY

Although not the biggest or longest Scottish river, the Spey is arguably the most well known. Running for 98 miles, it rises at over 300m at Loch Spey in the Monadhliath Mountains in the Scottish Highlands and eventually flows in a north-easterly direction to drain into the Moray Firth at Spey Bay.

The Spey is famous for two things: whisky and salmon! It has historically been one of Scotland's premier salmon fishing locations, and even has a cast named after it, which was developed to successfully cast on large rivers such as the Spey and the Welsh Wye. More than 50 whisky distilleries are found on Speyside, including Glenfiddich, Macallan and Glenfarclas. The abundance and quality of its water is the principal reason for the large number of whisky distilleries in the Speyside region. It takes roughly 50 litres of water to produce one litre of whisky.

The Spey has many tributaries, including the Avon, which is the largest, as well as the Dulnain, Feshie, Tromie, Truim, Fiddich, Nethy, Calder and Druie. By reputation, the Spey is the 'fastest-flowing river in Scotland', although this only really applies to the river of Grantown. From Grantown downstream to the river mouth at Tugnet, the gradient is high and uniform, with a 200m drop in altitude over a river distance of 45 miles. This means that, unlike most rivers, the further down you go, the more the pace of the river quickens.

The Spey passes through many towns including Craigellachie, Rothes, Aviemore, Grantown-on-Spey and Garmouth, to name a few. There are various walking routes, including the Speyside Way, which runs south-west from Buckie on the shore of the Moray Firth coast to Aviemore on the edge of the Cairngorm Mountains, a distance of approximately 65 miles.

RIVER TWEED

Forming part of the historic boundary between Scotland and England, the Tweed runs at 97 miles long, starting in the Lowther Hills at 725m above sea level, not far from the source of Scotland's other iconic lowland river, the Clyde. It snakes its way through the borders before entering Northumberland and joining the North Sea at Berwick-upon-Tweed.

Because of its cross-country course, the Tweed has a few rules (or lack thereof) that no other river in England has. For example, no rod licence is required to fish it. Given its location, it's no surprise that 'Tweed' is from the old Celtic for 'border'.

On the Scottish side, the river is often called the Tweed Water. The River Tweed was very important for the textile industry in the nineteenth century, as it provided power for all of the region's textile mills. Tweed cloth derives its name from this association.

The Tweed has numerous tributaries, including the River Till, Blackadder Water, Leithan Water, Manor Water, Gala Water, River Teviot and Quair Water. It passes through several towns on its way to the sea including Innerleithen, Peebles, Galashiels, Melrose, Kelso, Coldstream and Berwick-upon-Tweed.

There are a few walking routes with good views of the river to choose from including the Ninians Haugh and Hay Lodge Park walk in Peebles, which has an easy access path leading to bench seats and picnic tables along the riverside. At about three miles long, it's not a particularly arduous walk and takes you past Neidpath Castle, built in the twelfth century.

Towards the end of the Tweed, there are large gatherings of gulls, with rarer species such as yellow-legged gulls, Iceland gulls and ivory gulls occasionally joining them, especially in the winter.

Like many large rivers, the Tweed is host to a bombardment of invasive species as well, including American skunk cabbage, monkey flower and rhododendron.

RIVER DEE

There are five rivers in Great Britain with the name 'Dee' but the Scottish Dee is the longest at 81 miles, passing through Braemar and Aboyne before eventually finding the sea at Aberdeen. Starting up in the Cairngorms, it also has the honour of having the highest source of any major British river at 1,220m. It has a few tributaries, including the Lui, Gairn, Muick, Tanar and Feugh as well as Loch Muick, Lochs of Davan and Kinord, and the Loch of Skene.

'Dee' means 'goddess', derived from the Roman 'Deva', likely because of the river's divine associations, although it's unclear which goddess it was once linked with. The area has also long had a royal connection after Queen Victoria visited in 1848 and loved it so much that she and her husband, Prince Albert, built Balmoral Castle. The region between Braemar and Banchory is often called Royal Deeside.

There are many walks along the banks of the Dee, with some of its best being in the Cairngorms National Park. Try the Linn of Dee, which has a great selection of falls, gorges, fast water and breathtaking views. It's about a two-mile walk with a gradual incline, and has a car park managed by the National Trust for Scotland.

The Scottish Dee also flows near to many towns including Aboyne, Braemar, Banchory, Ballater, and finally Aberdeen. The city of Aberdeen derives its name from the river, which means 'mouth of the River Dee'. The estuary is home to many waders and attracts good numbers of bottlenose dolphins that come close to shore to hunt salmon returning up river. These are the largest bottlenose dolphins in the world, getting up to 4.5m long!

The Dee is also home to a nationally important population of pearl mussels, with one of the highest numbers of juveniles, meaning they are still successfully breeding here. The fast and relatively clean water helps these endangered molluscs, as well as the good numbers of trout and salmon that the mussels need to mature (see page 148).

Species spotlight

ARCTIC CHARR *Salvelinus alpinus*

Present in over 200 lochs, charr are spread across Scotland, though it may be a stretch to describe them as 'common'. Although they normally live in deep glacial lochs, some populations will enter rivers to spawn in the winter. This is actually how charr would have originally reached the lochs, as they would have once had a similar life cycle to salmon, living in rivers and then going to sea to grow larger. Then, over the last Ice Age, some of these charr got stuck in lochs when they became cut off from the rivers, and over the generations they shrank in size.

The male sports a stunning red belly, which is where the word 'charr' comes from, meaning 'red' in Gaelic. Charr can fill different niches according to what they feed on, with distinct groups forming in the same lochs. For example, some are benthic feeders and will feed predominantly on snails found on the bed, while others are more pelagic feeders and hunt in open water.

On average, they don't tend to grow much bigger than 20cm and are an important part of the food web for many large highland lochs, with species such as ferox trout (a form of large brown trout found in large lochs) specialising in eating them.

WHITE-TAILED EAGLE *Haliaeetus albicilla*

White-tailed eagles are the largest birds of prey in Britain, with a wingspan of up to 2.5m in length. Although often called sea eagles, they aren't strictly coastal and will move inland to feed and

nest. They pair up for life and build huge nests on cliffs or large trees, which they will often reuse. Around the salmon spawning season, they often patrol riverbanks, looking for dead and dying salmon to feed on.

The birds successfully bred on Rum in 1975 after reintroduction from Scandinavia following an absence of 70 years, having been driven to extinction in the UK. They favour carrion but will also take living prey, ranging from fish and geese to hares and even young deer. When they spot a fish with their tremendous eyesight, they glide down, reaching out their talons to grab the prey without landing, and carrying it off to a safe place to feed. When doing this, they can reach speeds of up to 70mph!

They are much broader-winged than the golden eagle, which can be found in the same areas. Adults have a pale head, yellow bill and, of course, a white tail, all of which golden eagles lack.

PEARL MUSSEL *Margaritifera margaritifera*

Pearl mussels are among the most incredible creatures found in British rivers. They need fast clean water to thrive and have long lifespans – exceeding 100 years for some of them. They need a few specific factors to flourish in rivers, including good numbers of trout and salmon. This is because when mussels reproduce, they emit clouds of little larvae called 'glochidia', which resemble tiny open mussels. In Pac-Man fashion, these glochidia swim into the water column and are inhaled by salmonids. Once inside the gills, they simply snap on and hitch a ride. As many as 5,000 of these little mussels can be found in a single fish (who apparently remain oblivious) and they latch on for at least six months until they have been carried upstream. Here, they drop off and anchor to the new riverbed. It's a very clever dispersal method for an otherwise sedentary animal, even if they do have to produce 200 million glochidia in a lifetime to make it worthwhile!

Pearls are made by pearl mussels as a natural defence against an irritant – such as a parasite – entering their shell and causing damage to their fragile body. The mussel slowly secretes layers of aragonite and conchiolin, materials that also make up its shell. Pearl mussels can also produce black pearls, which featured in the crown of Queen Victoria.

ATLANTIC SALMON *Salmo salar*

While salmon are found across the rest of the British Isles, Scotland has by far the most salmon rivers. The story of the salmon is an extraordinary one: born in a river where it will stay for up to three years (less in more food-abundant rivers like chalk streams), it then heads out to sea and journeys as far as the coast of Greenland, over 1,000 miles away. It returns after around four years, often to the same river it was born in, to breed. Unlike Pacific salmon, not all Atlantic salmon will die after spawning and around 10 per cent of females will repeat the process multiple times.

Salmon are a vital part of the nutrient cycle, particularly in Scottish rivers, which are often low in nutrients. They bring oils, protein and calcium up from the sea and, when they die, provide food for many species in and alongside the river, even helping bankside vegetation grow.

Some small male Atlantic salmon try their luck before going to sea and attempt to sneak in with a larger female when the dominant male is distracted. These are known as precocious parr.

SCOTTISH SPATE RIVERS

AMERICAN MINK *Neovison vison*

An import for the fur trade, mink were farmed in the UK from the 1920s. At their peak in the 1950s, there were 400 known fur farms in the UK and most likely some unofficial ones too.

American mink were first confirmed to be breeding in the wild in 1956, and by 1967 were present in over half the counties of England and Wales, and in much of lowland Scotland. During the 1990s, animal rights activists stormed many fur farms and released the mink, causing havoc (it should be noted mink were already well established in the wild by this time).

The trouble with mink is that they are very efficient hunters of bird nests, small fish and most notably water voles, almost single-handedly causing the voles' catastrophic decline. Otters have been linked to controlling numbers and are known to alter the mink's behaviour, with mink less bold in areas where otters are also present. This is largely because the otters don't want competition for resources. However, otters don't wipe mink out. Often mink trapping, as distasteful as it may sound, is the only solution to control these American marauders, and many ghillies, river keepers and estate managers use mink traps.

GOLDENEYE *Bucephala clangula*

Not to be mixed up with the James Bond film, this is a rather dapper-looking duck. Most goldeneyes are winter visitors to Britain, with around 21,000 birds arriving in the colder months. For the rest of the year, only a small breeding population of around 200 pairs remains in the Scottish Highlands. This is mostly concentrated along the River Spey, with scatterings across the rest of the country. It is one of the rarest breeding ducks in Britain and was only first recorded as a breeding species in 1970. Nest boxes account for most of the nest sites for this duck; without them, there would be very few breeding in Scotland.

From a distance, the goldeneye could be mixed up with the more common tufted duck, but it has a full-cheeked triangular head which in males is metallic green with a white spot between its signature golden eye and bill. Females are more subdued in colouration, with a grey back and a brown head.

This diving duck uses its powerful legs to swim underwater in search of small fish, mussels and insects. The male's impressive courtship display involves bending his head back as far as it will go until it touches the rump, while moving rapidly forward and kicking up water with his feet. Females respond with their own displays, most often with the 'head-forward' move.

PURPLE SAXIFRAGE *Saxifraga oppositifolia*

Higher up in the catchment, seeds of Arctic-alpine plants can be washed down from the cliffs high above, where they then grow at surprisingly low altitudes. Such species include purple saxifrage. This species is no stranger to cold conditions, being one of the most northerly growing species of flowering plant in the world, found on Kaffeklubben Island at the northern tip of Greenland.

It prefers limestone rock to hang down from, with damp crevices and cracks to attach to. An evergreen, its leaves are oval-shaped with pores dotted all over them. The flowers are stunning, each with five large petals of a deep pink or violet colour, and carpet the entire plant

The flowering season is during the spring and this is the only saxifrage that has purple flowers, so is easy to identify. Being a fairly early-blooming flower, it's an important source of nectar for the first insects to emerge in the spring, such as queen bumblebees and brimstone butterflies.

GOOSANDER *Mergus merganser*

The males and females of this saw-billed duck look drastically different. The male sports a dark green head with a blackish back and bright white breast. The female (below), on the other hand, has a gingery red head and slate grey body. Both have a red bill with a serrated edge to help them catch fish. The orange feet provide powerful propulsion when diving down in fast flows to catch small fish. They will sometimes work in small groups to corral fish into the margins for an easier meal.

Goosanders nest in tree holes, from which the young have to leap out in the spring. Unable to fly for some weeks, they stick close to the mother and hunt together.

Similar to the goldeneye, it has a comparatively recent history of breeding in Britain, first recorded in 1871. It built up numbers in Scotland and, since 1970, has spread across northern England into Wales, reaching south-west England. Another similar species is the red-breasted merganser, which is smaller and favours more coastal waters.

ORANGE-STRIPED STONEFLY *Perlodes mortoni*

This insect is rather special, as it's one of the few endemic species to the British Isles, only found in a handful of Scottish rivers and nowhere else in the world. It was previously thought to be the European species *Perlodes microcephalus* but has since been classified as a separate species.

The larvae prefer well-oxygenated water, and in warm weather they often congregate in the fast riffles. They take two years or more to reach maturity, unlike many of the smaller species of stonefly, which have a one-year life cycle.

As a larva, it's relatively easy to identify with its bright spattering of orange across the body (most other larger larvae are darker). The larvae can grow up to 3cm long and have a powerful set of jaws for crushing up other small aquatic insects.

As an adult, it retains its flattened body shape and outward-angled legs but the orange is largely absent, with only faint hints of it lingering on the head. Males have relatively short wings compared to the females. They emerge from the rivers from March to June.

FLAT-HEADED MAYFLIES *Heptageniidae spp*

The adult form of these river flies is fairly typical of the mayfly order, with wings closed above the back, a fat abdomen and three long tail bristles. It's the larvae that are really interesting, being quite different in appearance and habits to other mayfly larvae. They are built for life in fast-flowing water with a horizontally compressed body profile, meaning the water just runs off their backs. This enables them to move with relative ease, even in the fastest flows, as well as slide between the smallest cracks to find food and shelter that other species can't. They have small sharp hooks on each of their six legs to grip onto rocks, and they graze on the algae growing on them.

There is one generation a year, which usually overwinters as larvae and emerges between April and July, although sometimes as late as September or October. There are around 11 flat-headed mayfly species in Britain, which are very difficult to tell apart when larvae but easier when they develop into the adult forms. They require large amounts of oxygenated water and so they need fast-flowing water for their survival; they are rarely found in slower-moving water.

10

Ponds

Although we tend to think of ponds and rivers as being distinct and separate types of waterbody (and of course in most situations they are), the two are very closely linked. Over millennia, rivers will slowly creep into bends, meanders and curls which, over time, can be cut off from the main river. There are also channels and depressions that are still connected to the river but the flow has stopped going into them, making them, for all intents and purposes, ponds.

Many ponds can become isolated, but the wildlife that lives in ponds thrives best when there's a network of ponds to utilise. This is where rivers come in. The river and its wet margins act like a freshwater motorway, allowing creatures to travel from one pond to another under relative safety and damp conditions.

While there's no officially accepted classification, as a rule of thumb anything smaller than 2 hectares is referred to as a pond, while any larger bodies of water are considered lakes.

← A common frog sits on a lily pad in a duckweed-covered pond.

↑ Ponds, either human-made or natural, found near rivers are biodiversity hotspots that help many specialised species find a home.

Pond creation

Sometimes ponds are created in fairly simple ways, for example a large fallen tree may dam up a section of smaller river. The roots and soil that are lifted up often leave a large hole, which can also create a second small pond.

If beavers are present on the river, they will create ponds, interconnected via small trickles and streams. Something as simple as a deer wallow, where large deer press into the ground to cover themselves in mud, can also become a shallow pond, as the ground eventually hardens and holds water. This also happens in areas with wild boar, but deer are far more widespread in Britain.

While many people have garden ponds, in more recent years organisations have started creating ponds next to rivers and river valleys to help reduce flooding and increase biodiversity. They act as a sponge, drawing in excess water when the rivers are in high flow. When rivers are re-meandered (see also page 28), ponds are often also included in the planning, with several added along the course of the new river.

Pond lifespan

It's important to note that ponds come in many shapes and forms and many have a limited lifespan. Ponds will often get covered by reeds and marginal plants, creating a wet boggy area which, in time, can dry out to make way for small trees and shrubs. The time this process takes varies wildly, sometimes just a few years while, in other cases, ponds can be around for hundreds of years before drying out.

Ponds don't always dry out; they may be cleared out artificially by people, or naturally by herbivorous species such as swans, deer and water voles, which help keep the plants at bay. The bottom can also be dug out by species such as beavers and some fish, like carp, will root around the bottom of a pond and create huge feeding holes.

When pond and river meet

Many creatures will be specialised for ponds and still waters, so having ponds next to a river creates a melting pot of riverine and pond species. Around two-thirds of Britain's wetland plants and wildlife can be found in and around ponds so, for a relatively small habitat, one pond can support a great diversity of life.

Each pond will have its own zones, with warm shallow margins and deeper cooler water towards the centre. Lots of rocks and logs can create hiding spots for aquatic insects, including caddisfly and dragonfly larvae. The long reeds provide a landing pad for adult dragonflies and a pit stop for reed warblers.

Ponds with thick weeds have plenty of space for amphibians to lay eggs, while more open ponds have a clear pathway for pond skaters and whirligig beetles. Generally, the more aquatic plants present in a pond, the clearer the water is – although other factors include the pond's size, whether there is an inflow to it, and the amount of sunlight. The bottom is often a mix of mud, silt and plant matter, meaning the slightest movement will stir it up into a cloud of mud.

Some ponds are also connected via small outlets and feeder streams to rivers, which help maintain water levels in the warmer months and provide a direct pathway for species to enter them.

Pit stop

Wildlife, including amphibians, certain invertebrates and water voles, will all use rivers as a watery highway and then split off into nearby ponds where they can rest up before moving on. The ponds act as vital service stations for many species and help various creatures colonise new water bodies.

Flooding can also translocate species into riverside ponds, including eels, which may well prefer a quiet pond to fatten up in and, being so long-lived, can simply wait for the next flood to re-enter the river. While fish are at the mercy of floods, other animals can take a more deliberate route. Most adults of aquatic insects can fly, with 3,000 species of diving beetle in Britain hiding wings under their armoured case. Dragonflies will also scout out new ponds to lay eggs in.

The biodiversity is always higher when there's a network of ponds. Each pond can have its own subtle little ecosystem with different depths, temperatures, plant life and level of sunlight, which will affect which species call it home.

Fish eggs on duck's feet?

There are many cases of fish ending up in remote ponds, and a popular theory for how they got there is that fish eggs get stuck to the feet of ducks, which then deposit them into the pond. I hate to burst the bubble but this is incredibly unlikely. Fish eggs are very sensitive to light, temperature and drying out so, unless the pond is very close, this simply wouldn't happen. However there is another possible explanation involving ducks. In a study carried out by the

→ Large-grooved diving beetle.

Centre for Ecological Research in Debrecen, Hungary, carp eggs were fed to mallards and it was found that about 0.2 percent of ingested eggs – 18 of 8,000 – were still intact after defecation. So the chances are low, but not impossible, for fish eggs to be moved around by ducks in this way. I, however, take a far more cynical viewpoint and think that if fish turn up in a remote pond, it's generally more likely to be someone dumping discarded pets or wanting to set up a new fishing spot!

Amphibians in need

Ponds are vital lifelines for amphibians, of which we have seven native species in Britain. They use ponds to breed, mostly in spring, as well as to hibernate, feed and take shelter in drier periods of the year.

Three of the seven native species are protected: the natterjack toad, great crested newt (see page 164) and pool frog (see page 163), all of which have a limited distribution. Among the biggest threats to amphibians are fungal diseases, in particular, chytrid. The chytrid fungus infects the skin of amphibians, disrupting its normal function, which is critical for respiration and moisture regulation. Infected amphibians may

↓ Ducks gathering by a pond.   ↑ Common frog.

die from dehydration or electrolyte imbalance, as their skin's ability to exchange gases and regulate water is compromised. While it is present in Britain, chytrid is wreaking havoc in more humid tropical locations across the world, and has been linked to the extinction or severe population declines of many species, particularly frogs.

Some species like pool and marsh frogs are more resistant, as their habit of basking allows UV light to kill off the fungus. If you keep pet amphibians, it's incredibly important not to release them into the wild to help curb the spread of the fungus.

Adding to your own pond

If you are considering collecting plants from the wild to add to your own pond, there are a few things to consider.

Firstly, aquatic plants will colonise ponds on their own, although it may take a while, especially if you don't live near other ponds.

It's generally a good idea to only collect from ponds that are near to you, ideally within 10 miles, as they will be adapted to the local climate. It also helps to avoid spreading species that are not already present in the local area. Be wary when buying plants from a garden centre, as they are often mislabelled and can carry some non-native hitchhikers that you may accidentally introduce to your pond and local environment.

I'd recommend putting any new plants into a bucket of water for a week or so before planting them into your pond, so you can spot and remove anything you don't want in the pond that may have tagged along.

Embrace your inner artist

Although photography is my main profession, I would hesitate to call myself an artist. When you see people connect paint and brush, real magic can happen, and the river is a great place to let those creative juices flow, offering a beautiful and peaceful location to indulge in a relaxing hobby.

It doesn't matter if you're not the next Claude Monet. I think it's a case of just finding an outlet to explore a new creative endeavour and see what it brings. Next time you're sitting by the riverbank, why not take a pen and paper (or other materials) and just see whether inspiration strikes?

↓ Selecting a healthy waterlily root to transplant to a garden pond.

TIPS FOR OUTDOOR ART

- Be mindful that you won't be in a warm studio, so **be prepared for the elements** and, of course, nosy people passing by!
- **Why not combine interests** and use your art as a way of recording what species you have seen?
- Many people prefer to keep their art to themselves, but **if you do want to share it, there are plenty of social media outlets** for wildlife art and many nature centres offer free exhibitions.
- **Don't begrudge yourself the downtime.** It's sometimes healthy to just be on your own, indulging in whatever your preferred pastime or hobby is, and giving yourself a reason to be outdoors.

↑ Southern hawker.

Hunt for dragons

While there are plenty of riverside dragonflies and damselflies, most species are found on ponds and lakes, so if you have an area with both running water and ponds, you can really stack up an impressive list of sightings of these incredible insects.

Dragonflies have been on earth for 300 million years, with some of their ancient relatives reaching lengths of 60cm! We have 50 or so species of odonates (the collective term for dragonflies and damselflies). Some species can emerge from April, such as the large red damselfly, while others, such as common darter, will still be flying around as late as December. The best time to see as many as possible is July to August, when most of the larger dragonflies will be on the wing.

Don't forget to check stems poking out of the water – you may be lucky and find an exuvia, the shed skin of a larva that has emerged. I like to take a notepad to write down the species I see, (or you can do the same on a phone) and take pictures of the species I'm not sure about so I can identify them when I get home.

SUCCESSFUL SPOTTING

- **Warm days are best** for seeing dragonflies in flight. Around midday they will be at peak activity, hawking for prey.
- **Early morning is also a good time** to look for dragonflies and damselflies, as you may find some of them resting on plants and waiting for the sun, which allows you a close-up look.
- Although mainly associated with water, dragonflies will forage quite a long way from water so **check out meadows and parks too.**
- Individuals often have a favourite spot they return to, so **if you spot a dragonfly sitting on a branch, keep an eye out** as it may well return to it later on.
- **Bring binoculars** – people think they are only for birds but they are really useful for the larger species of dragonfly as well.

Pond profiles

FARM PONDS

The farm pond was once a crucial part of rural life and it would have been fairly standard to have multiple ponds in one field. These days, they are still around, but in far fewer numbers.

Historically, they would have watered livestock and were a convenient way to water crops. They were also used to house waterfowl and fish as an easy source of food. These ponds were home to the crucian (see page 163), a small member of the carp family, and the original strain of common carp, sometimes known as wild carp. Carp are very hardy and will live quite well in small muddy ponds, breeding prolifically.

Farm ponds are normally formed in a bowl shape to maximise the amount of water they can store and to help with the irrigation of crops when needed. The location needs to be just right, generally in the lowest-lying part of the farm so that water will naturally travel to this spot and collect at the pond. In the past, farm ponds would sometimes also be created accidentally when an area was mined for clay or marl and a pond formed at the extraction site.

These ponds are vital pit stops for many aquatic creatures traversing the farmland landscape, and provide a quiet haven for more sensitive and shy species, as they are often on private land where footfall is very low. These could be yellowhammers coming down for a drink or cattle egrets stalking pond edges looking for a small frog.

More than half a million ponds have been lost in the UK over the last 100 years, which is an astonishing number. Some become ghost ponds, drying out over time when trees creep in and suck up all the moisture, and some have been filled back in with topsoil. These days, there are various efforts to reclaim lost ponds by digging them out and allowing nature to take hold again.

↓ Small weedy ponds are perfect for all kinds of creatures such as dragonflies, crucians and newts.

OXBOW LAKES

An oxbow lake is a U-shaped lake that forms when a wide meander of a river is cut off, creating a free-standing body of water. 'Oxbow' can also refer to any U-shaped bend in a river or stream, whether or not it is cut off from the main stream. The name derives from its similarity to a piece of metal traditionally used on an ox's yoke. In Britain, oxbow lakes can be found on a few of the larger river systems, for example at Cuckmere Haven in Sussex and Butterby Oxbow in Durham, but are not especially common.

Oxbows are often created during a flood event. Over time, the river continues to erode the outer edge of the meander and deposit sediment on the inner edge, narrowing the neck of the meander. Eventually, during a high-water event or flood, the river may breach the narrow neck of the meander and create a new, straighter path. Once the river takes the shortcut, the old meander becomes cut off from the main flow of water. This remaining curved section is the oxbow lake.

These natural bodies of still water support a wide array of wildlife that would otherwise struggle in the flowing water, including dragonflies, amphibians and soft-bodied pond plants. They also act as an important stepping stone to other ponds for creatures to colonise and, when a river floods, are an important bolt hole for fish to escape the faster flows.

Oxbows are more common on lowland rivers with a slower flow that won't erode the bank when an oxbow is created. They generally have a limited lifespan. Over time, they may fill with sediment and organic matter, becoming shallower and eventually transforming into marshes or dry land.

↓ Oxbow in Cuckmere Valley, East Sussex.

↑ One of the ponds on the pingo trail in the Brecks, Norfolk.

PINGOS

The award to best name for a water body has to go to … the pingo! It comes from the Inuit word for 'hill', which might seem strange to apply to a pond, but there is a reason. Pingos were created at the end of the last Ice Age and have been left almost untouched since. As the glaciers retreated, these icy hills melted and they left hard lenses of ice pressed into the ground with soil over the top of them. When temperatures rose, this caused the ice to melt, forming a depression filled with water – a pingo pond. Pingos are a key indicator of permafrost conditions. Their presence suggests that the area has had a history of permafrost, giving us a glimpse into the past.

Pingos are a very rare type of pond, with the largest density in Britain being in the Brecks in Norfolk, where they are also known as kettle lakes. Elsewhere in Britain, most pingos have been ploughed up. In Norfolk there's a pingo trail you can walk, which is just under eight miles long, taking you through spots such as Thompson Common. The common is one of the most important sites in the county for dragonflies and damselflies and a visit in July and early August offers an amazing spectacle with huge numbers of dragonflies filling the air. A wide variety of species of butterflies and beetles have also been found here.

The pingo trail walk is mostly flat, and there are several small car parks along it. While many of the pingos are hidden away, some are accessible to the public, and what's fascinating is how so many ponds so close to each other can each have their own look, shape and ecosystem, with different plants dominating different ponds. These pond networks create a fantastic and diverse habitat for many creatures to inhabit, and pingos are home to many species such as pond mud snails, pool frogs, water beetles and great crested newts.

TEMPORARY PONDS

Many ponds will eventually dry out. While this can cause concern for many people, some creatures actually thrive in these temporary or vernal pools.

Natterjack toads, for instance, like to lay their eggs in these ponds because any potential predators of the tadpoles, like fish or dragonfly larvae, are less likely to become established. This means the tadpoles are safer, although they have to metamorphose at an astonishing rate, hatching within a week and leaving the pond after six weeks, compared to common toads, which take 16 weeks on average.

As they tend to be shallow, these ponds are also much warmer, which suits some very rare and ancient creatures. In a couple of sites in Britain such as the New Forest and Caerlaverock, we get tadpole shrimps or *Triops*, which look a bit like miniature horseshoe crabs. They have a quick life cycle, taking only a month or so to develop from egg to adult. The eggs are triggered to hatch by warmth and water and can stay hidden and dry for years. They aren't fussy, and will eat anything they come across in the pond.

Some temporary ponds, also known as ephemeral or seasonal ponds, exist for only part of the year, typically during the wet or rainy season, returning each year if the conditions are right. These ponds often support specialised plant communities that can tolerate periods of drought and fluctuating water levels, for example certain species of water lilies, mosses and aquatic grasses. Scrapes are another kind of temporary pond, which are very shallow but often quite wide. They are popular with waders foraging for food, who use their bills to poke into the soft mud and find worms.

There are also instances of temporary ponds created by human activity. For example, on the Ministry of Defence land on Salisbury Plain, the tracks left by tanks cause small puddles, which can become ponds for a while and support a few species (although they have to avoid tanks every now and then!).

↑ Natterjack toad.
← Tadpole shrimp.

Species spotlight

CRUCIAN *Carassius carassius*

Also known as a crucian carp, this species is closely related to the common carp. These buttery gold-coloured fish are pond specialists, thriving in small, heavily weeded ponds. Although they all have a generally rounded appearance, the body shape can vary depending on the presence of other predatory fish. Larger water bodies that contain pike and eels produce more high-backed and rounded crucians, which is thought to be a hormonal response to make them harder to swallow.

Crucians are perfectly designed for life in a pond, having circular fins for slow movement and a strong tolerance for water that is low in oxygen, which during the winter can be very beneficial. The crucian has a novel way of surviving in ponds that often freeze over and would kill other fish – it gets drunk! Crucians have evolved a set of enzymes that convert lactic acid to alcohol, which stops them from freezing and can then be easily removed from the body via their gills. The recorded blood alcohol levels in crucians have exceeded 50mg per 100 millilitres, which is the same as the drink-drive limit in Scotland.

Crucians are in decline across Europe, largely due to hybridisation with Gibel carp, goldfish and common carp, all of which are closely related and quickly breed the crucians out of existence. Small farm ponds are isolated and therefore a lifeline for these beautiful fish.

POOL FROG *Pelophylax lessonae*

This stunning little amphibian is one of only two native frog species in Britain (along with the common frog), though it was once thought to be non-native. By the time people realised that it was indeed native, in the 1990s, the frog was almost extinct, down to one lone male at Thompson Common in Norfolk. Pool frogs from Sweden, deemed to be a close genetic match, were released into a couple of sites in Norfolk and have since started a stable population. There are other populations across England, though many of these are likely from southern Europe and probably originate from escaped or dumped pets.

Unlike common frogs, the pool frog spends most of its time either in or next to the water. The colouration varies, from bright green to a mixture of browns, blacks and yellows. It has a loud call, sounding a bit like a mallard. To escape danger, pool frogs can jump great distances of over a metre (much more than a common frog), normally straight into the water.

They are also sun worshippers, often basking in the warm sun while they wait for unsuspecting prey to crawl by.

While pool frogs are fairly easy to distinguish from common frogs, there are other water frogs, in particular the introduced marsh frog, with which it could get confused. Typically marsh frogs are much bigger, up to 18cm in body length, and much louder.

GREAT SILVER WATER BEETLE *Hydrophilus piceus*

The great silver water beetle takes the title for the heaviest beetle in Britain. Largely restricted to the south of England, it is fairly uncommon and typically found in ditches and dykes with vegetation to hide away in. The larva is arguably even more impressive, reaching lengths of 7cm and primarily feeding on aquatic snails. The adult switches diet to plant matter and moves around thick vegetation, gently grazing. Its back legs, with feather-like strands, are used to propel it forward in the water and, although not often seen in flight, it can indeed fly from one water body to another, which is how it colonises new ponds.

It is unlikely to be confused with other British diving beetles due to its size, unique silver-looking colouration and behaviour of coming to the water's surface head-first (others collect air from the surface bottom-first!).

GREAT CRESTED NEWT *Triturus cristatus*

The largest newt species in Britain, great crested newts can reach lengths of 16cm. The skin is black with numerous bumps across it, giving it its other name: the warty newt. The belly varies between fiery red and pale yellow, with black blotches that are unique to each newt. Only the male has a crest, as well as a patch of white along his tail.

During the breeding season, if the male fails to impress a female with his crest, he has a more flamboyant way to attract her attention: he dances. The male positions himself in front of the female, arches his back and wriggles his tail seductively. If she is impressed, he'll release a packet of sperm for her to collect. Over the next few months, she'll lay the eggs – up to 200 – individually on plants.

These newts are top predators of ponds, devouring anything they come across. They can take prey as large as sticklebacks and smooth newts and will demolish frog tadpoles. They tend to stay in the pond for the spring before heading out onto land to find a damp patch to hide away and find food, normally small worms, beetles and slugs.

One reason for their decline is that they require a network of ponds, which are becoming increasingly scarce, to maintain a decent-sized population, with enough space to spread out and find enough food.

GREATER BLADDERWORT *Utricularia vulgaris*

This unassuming water plant may look harmless but is in fact deadly – if you're a daphnia that is. This plant can live in nutrient-poor ponds by using a special way to get what it needs – it is a carnivore. The bladderwort has a series of 'bladders' or small pouches along its stem which suck up and trap passing insects. The insect will slowly die and is digested over time.

The plant doesn't root to the bottom of the pond and is a good oxygenator. It produces a simple yellow flower from July to August. Aside from its pouches, it looks similar to hornwort.

During the winter, the plant grows brittle and sinks to the bottom of the pond before rising up again in the spring.

It can spread quickly and is not a rare species, but tends to be locally abundant in slightly acidic waters.

There is another species called the yellow bladderwort from which it can only be reliably distinguished when in flower. If there are developing or ripe seed capsules on the plant, then it's greater bladderwort. Yellow bladderwort is sterile and does not produce any seed capsules.

NORFOLK HAWKER *Aeshna isoceles*

One of the most striking dragonfly species in Britain is the Norfolk hawker. Brown in overall appearance, it has striking green eyes and clear wings, separating it from the brown hawker, which has blue or brown eyes and amber-coloured wings.

It gets its name from its historical distribution of the Broadlands of Norfolk and north-east Suffolk but in recent decades has expanded its range to include Kent, Dorset and even as far north as Yorkshire. It's thought a warming climate has helped with its expansion. It's a protected species and it is an offence to harm or disturb it.

Norfolk hawkers like a series of interconnecting dykes, ponds and reed-fringed margins where they can rest and stalk prey. They are on the wing from May to August, with sunny days best to see them 'hawking' for prey. Mornings are best to see them stationary as they bask in the sun to warm up. One of their favourite plants to lay eggs on is the water soldier.

Like many larger dragonflies, the Norfolk hawker will patrol and fiercely defend its territory from other dragonflies, showcasing some incredible aerial acrobatics.

DAUBENTON'S BAT *Myotis daubentonii*

Although most of the 18 or so species of bat that call Britain home will use ponds to catch insects, the Daubenton's bat takes it to the next level.

With a body only 5cm long, it is a tiny but proficient hunter. Using echolocation, it can detect small insects trapped on the surface of the water and will swoop in, using its hind legs to scoop the prey up into its mouth. This has led to its other name, the water bat, as it almost exclusively feeds by water bodies.

The fur is short and reddish-brown with a paler grey belly. The ears are relatively short and the face can appear pink, with bare patches around the eyes. It has large feet, relative to its size, which help it grab prey.

The Daubenton's bat is currently expanding its range across Great Britain, which could be because of the increasing number of artificial lakes and large garden ponds. Like all British bats, it hibernates during the winter, typically in caves, tunnels and old mines, but also holes in trees and gaps in buildings.

WATER RAIL *Rallus aquaticus*

Although a fairly abundant bird, the water rail is quite secretive and rarely seen. It is in the same family as moorhens and crakes, but has a longer and more slender bill for picking out invertebrates in the mud. The plumage is a mottled light brown with a grey head and belly, and the bill is red. The young chicks are jet black and very fluffy. Pairs produce a couple of broods a year.

Its favoured habitat is thick reeds and bulrushes where it can hide away. It is more often heard than seen, making a noise known as 'sharming', which sounds like a pig squealing.

The best time to see a water rail is in the winter when the reeds are thinning out and cold weather may bring it out in the open. Often a frost is a good time, as it can be seen walking on the ice.

It has a fairly wide distribution across the British Isles, from tiny ponds to estuaries. As long as there are reeds for it to hide away in, there's a chance that any pond is home to one of these shy birds.

RAFT SPIDER *Dolomedes fimbriatus*

The raft spider is one of the largest native spiders in Britain, with its body reaching lengths of 2cm, and females (which are bigger than the males) reaching 7cm when including the legs.

Unlike most spiders, the raft spider doesn't use a web to hunt prey. Instead, it rests its legs, which have special waterproof hairs, on the water's surface and grabs prey as it passes. If needed, it can dive down below the water to escape predators and even hunt prey such as fish, tadpoles and dragonfly larvae.

The raft spider has a preference for acidic ponds, and is found in environments such as heathland, bogs and moorland ponds. It can be found in the very north of Scotland and the south coast of England, but interestingly is all but absent in the areas between them.

The body is brown overall, with two broad white stripes down its back, so it is relatively easy to distinguish from terrestrial spiders. There is a slightly larger relative called the great fen raft spider but this is only found in a handful of sites in East Anglia.

FLOWERING RUSH *Butomus umbellatus*

Despite the name, this is not actually a member of the rush family but is instead in its own distinct family: Butomaceae.

The flowering rush reaches up to 1m and has thin, sword-like leaves. It has a collection of pretty pink petals with an umbel-like stalk housing the individual flowers. It is an important plant for pollination for many pondside invertebrates. It's most easily seen in the summer from July to August when it's in full bloom, as it blends in with other rush-like plants during the rest of the year. It spreads via its rhizomes, but the seeds do also sometimes disperse after flowering.

Although it can be found in riverbank margins, it's more commonly associated with small ponds, where it prefers damp, fertile soils in full sun. It is found at a range of depths and can push out into deeper water, before dying back in the winter. It can be planted in garden ponds.

The other common names for flowering rush include the grassy rush, lily grass and water gladiolus. It was once locally called 'pride of the Thames' but sadly, persistent dredging and bankside erosion have meant it has all but disappeared from the River Thames, though it is found on nearby ponds and lakes.

River Pubs

There's no finer tradition than visiting the great British pub, and a riverside pub is often a cut above the rest, allowing you to watch kingfishers zoom by while you enjoy a nice cold drink. While I could have done an entirely separate book on this subject, here is a short list of some fantastic riverside pubs that I've painstakingly researched and visited!

ANGLERS REST, Derbyshire

This charming pub is a hidden gem in the Peak District, offering a stop-off for a much-needed drink along the Monsal Trail. The Derbyshire Wye passes right in front of it and you can often see dippers. Built in 1753, the pub has a log fire and plenty of snugs to warm up after a long walk. It has plenty of tasty real ales and locally sourced food, and the riverside beer garden is a must-visit!

Location: Buxton, Derbyshire (SK17 8SN)
Local Drink: Peak Ales Chatsworth Gold 4.6%
Parking: Yes
Food: Yes
Dog Friendly: Yes
Accommodation: Yes

COMPLEAT ANGLER, Norwich

Named after the famous seventeenth-century book, the Compleat Angler sits on the River Wensum, surrounded by moorings and with plenty of seating for al fresco drinking and dining. Otters have been seen passing the pub, and some huge pike lurk near the moorings. Found in the heart of Norwich, close to the train station and Norwich Cathedral, it's an easy pub to reach and grab a pint.

Location: Norwich, Norfolk (NR1 1NS)
Local Drink: Woodforde's Bure Gold 4.0%
Parking: Not on site but plenty of city parking nearby
Food: Yes
Dog Friendly: Yes
Accommodation: No

CRESSELLY ARMS, Pembrokeshire

This 250-year-old pub welcomes visitors with a large sign saying no dogs or children, which, depending on your situation, is either a curse or a blessing! Regularly voted one of the best country pubs in Wales, it sits on the banks of the Cresswell River, which is tidal at this stretch. It has a large beer garden where you can enjoy the views of the river valley and great local beers. It's a Grade II-listed traditional pub with roaring fires and ivy-covered walls. There are multiple walking routes that lead to it, as well as mooring nearby for boaters.

Location: Cresswell Quay, Pembrokeshire (SA68 0TE)
Local Drink: Bluestone Rocketeer 4.6%
Parking: Yes
Food: Not on site, but food vendors appear throughout the year
Dog Friendly: No (nor child-friendly!), apart from outside
Accommodation: No

KINGS ARMS, York

Perhaps best known as 'the pub that floods', it gets submerged four times a year on average, and before the River Ouse got too contaminated it would remain open for locals to grab a beer even while flooded! Because of the river's habit of creeping into the pub, all electrics and beer are housed upstairs. The pub also has a digital detox rule, banning all phones, laptops or other devices to encourage people to simply talk to each other.

Location: York, Yorkshire (YO1 9SN)
Local Drink: Black Sheep Amber Ale 4.4%
Parking: Not on site, but plenty of city parking nearby
Food: No
Dog Friendly: Yes
Accommodation: No

→ The Mayfly Inn on the River Test.

MAYFLY INN, Test Valley

This iconic riverside pub sits on the banks of the River Test, with the river flowing through the beer garden. Plenty of hungry trout wait nearby for a spare chip or bit of bread to be thrown in. If you time your visit right, you could see an explosion of mayflies hatching. In the colder months, a log fire is located in the bar ready to warm up chilly travellers. The pub is also on the National Cycle Network.

Location: Stockbridge, Hampshire (SO20 6AX)
Local Drink: Steam Town West Coast IPA 5.4%
Parking: Yes
Food: Yes
Dog Friendly: Yes
Accommodation: No

ROCKFORD INN, Devon

Hidden away in a deep, wooded Exmoor valley and overlooking the dramatic East Lyn river, this cosy, low-beamed pub is more than 400 years old and offers home-cooked food and a log fire. Permits from the pub are available to fish for salmon and sea trout. There are also some great walking routes into Exmoor.

Location: Lynton, Devon (EX35 6PT)
Local Drink: Exmoor Cider 4.8%
Parking: Yes
Food: Yes
Dog Friendly: Yes
Accommodation: Yes

TAYBANK, Dunkeld

The stunning River Tay passes this pub, which boasts the largest beer garden in Perthshire. They often have events on, such as live music and outdoor cinema screenings. Built in 1809, the hotel is an ideal stop-off for a bite to eat or a drink or two. You can go fishing for salmon outside the hotel, paddle downstream or simply go for a walk on one of the many trails in the area. Note: the indoor bar is for residents only.

Location: Dunkeld, Perthshire (PH8 0AQ)
Local Drink: Blair Athol 12-year-old Single Malt Whisky 43%
Parking: Yes
Food: Yes
Dog Friendly: Yes
Accommodation: Yes

TRENT LOCK PUB, Sawley

The pub gets its name from the nearby Trent Lock, which, as well as marking the point where the River Trent and River Soar meet with the beginning of the Erewash Canal, also sits on the border of three counties: Leicestershire, Nottinghamshire and Derbyshire. Easily accessible by boat, bike or car, it's a perfect pub to visit on a sunny summer afternoon, with ample outside seating by the river – although the garden can get busy. Boaters can moor close to the pub.

Location: Long Eaton, Derbyshire (NG10 2FY)
Local Drink: Blue Monkey Cinder Toffee Stout 5%
Parking: Yes
Food: Yes
Dog Friendly: Yes, treats ready at the bar!
Accommodation: No

River Names

Every single piece of running water in Great Britain has a name, and they all mean something. Whether it is to do with the strength of a river, its colour or its shape, the name gives you a clue to the river's past, with most names having roots in Celtic, Pictish and Norse.

Some names are local to a specific county and others are specific to an individual river. Some rivers share the same name, such as Ouse, Avon and Stour. In fact we have five River Avons in England, three in Scotland and one in Wales, so it's a popular name! Often the names are an old word for 'water' or 'river' so they are essentially called 'River River'. River names can be a fantastic window into the past as a river tends to retain its original name, and even if it changes slightly over the centuries, the linguistic roots are still there.

Here are some of our rivers and the meanings behind their names, followed by the meanings and origins behind some of the regional terms for different types of river or features of a river. For a list of more general terms, see the glossary on page 172.

↑ The River Nidd (meaning 'brilliant river') at Knaresborough.

Modern Names and Meanings

Avon: river, water
Cerne, Char: stony river
Clyst, Clyde: cleansing one
Darent, Dart, Derwent: oak-fringed stream
Dee, Don, Doon: river of the goddess
Devon, Dowlas: black river
Earn: blowing
Eden: gushing
Ellen: holy
Esk, Exe, Usk: water
Forth: slow river
Frome: fair river
Glyme: bright stream
Humber: good
Kennet: regal
Leven, Leam, Lynn: elm river
Lochy: dark river
Lossie: herb river
Nene: bright river
Nidd: brilliant river
Ouse: water
Oykel: high
Pant: valley
Stour: large, powerful (adjective) or tumult, commotion (noun)
Taf: water
Tamar, Team, Thame, Teme, Thames: water or dark river
Tarff: charging like a bull
Tay: powerful
Tees: surging
Test: swift, strong
Trent: trespasser, strongly flooding
Tyne: water
Ure: holy
Wear, Welland: river
Wey, Wye: flowing
Wyre: winding

Regional Terms

aber: Pictish for 'river mouth', used in areas in Scotland and Wales

afon: Welsh for 'river' (the origin of the many Avons in England)

beck: a small stream with a stony bed or following a rugged course, mainly used in northern England

bourne: intermittent stream in chalk, mainly in southern England

broads: interconnecting rivers within Norfolk

burn: small stream or river, normally used in Scotland but also north-west England

carrier: often a human-made offshoot of a chalk stream, particularly on the Itchen or Test

cleugh: gorge that is the course of a stream on a steep-sided river valley in Scotland

delph: fenland river

dumble: local term used in Nottinghamshire to describe a wood-lined stream, often in a small, steep-sided valley

eau: term used in Lincolnshire, coming from old English for 'river'

ffrwd: 'stream' in Welsh

ghyll or **gill:** ravine or narrow valley, used in Cumbria and parts of lowland Scotland

gleeb: marshy stream, thought to originate from *gwlyb* ('wet') in Welsh

goit: regional name for a small river in Yorkshire

grain: Scottish borders term to describe a river that forks or splits

gutter: regional name for a small river in the New Forest

hope: Scottish borders term to describe an enclosed upland river

leat: waterways designed to feed other waterways, or to supply water-powered mills and industries. Common in south and west England and Wales

letch: offshoots of the Tyne found in boggy land

linn: waterfall or torrent of rushing water in a river or stream, mainly Scottish

lode: short, straight stretch of water, normally connecting a village to a major river. Often used in Cambridgeshire. From Old English meaning 'way' or 'course'

loup: river in Scotland with many waterfalls or leaps, named after salmon trying to leap the falls

nant: short Welsh river

pill: localised to the Severn Estuary, refers to deep tidal water offshoots from the main Severn

pow: slow-moving stream

sike or **syke:** Scottish borders term to describe a small river that flows through boggy ground

tyne: generally used to refer to smaller source streams or rivulets in Scotland. Thought to originate from the Gaelic 'teann' meaning 'tight and fixed' in reference to the river's small nature

↓ The River Avon, Bristol. Eight other rivers in Britain share the same name.

Glossary

aquifer: chalk filter that water rises from underground to create a chalk stream

babble or **burble:** small river with a loud watercourse of rushing water over shallow rocks

backwater: part of a river not reached by the current, where the water is stagnant

brook: small stream

channel: wide strait or waterway between two landmasses that lie close to each other

creek: narrow, sheltered waterway, especially an inlet in a shoreline or channel in a marsh

ditch: steep-sided, often human-made watercourse used for excess water

drain: human-made channel, often very straight and used for irrigation

flume: human-made channel for water, in the form of an open declined gravity chute whose walls are raised above the surrounding terrain, in contrast to a trench or ditch

headwater: the start of a river

meander: single channel winding snake-like through a valley

mere: shallow water body, normally still water but can have mild flow

mill race: channel carrying the swift current of water that drives a mill wheel

mill stream: artificial watercourse or aqueduct dug into the ground, especially one supplying water to a watermill

reach: any length of river or stream

riffle: gentle course of water, often shallow and over gravel

ril or **rillet:** small river

rindle: small (usually fordable) stream

rivulet: small stream

run: area where the water is flowing rapidly, generally located downstream from riffles

runnel: fast-moving small river

seep: low-volume spring

spring: natural exit point at which groundwater emerges from the aquifer and flows onto the top of the earth's crust

tributary: side stream from a main river

watercourse: general term for a body of water, often in regard to navigation

waterway: general term for moving water body

↓ Rivers can be open and cold places in winter, so remember to wrap up warm.

Organisations

Here is a selection of charities and groups that are involved in the restoration, protection and promotion of British rivers and their wildlife. Many of them offer volunteering opportunities if you'd like to get involved.

ANGLING TRUST,
anglingtrust.net
A not-for-profit organisation representing anglers, fighting for fish, fishing and the environment.

CANAL & RIVER TRUST,
canalrivertrust.org.uk
A charity that cares for 2,000 miles of canals, rivers, docks and reservoirs.

GRAYLING SOCIETY,
graylingsociety.net
A not-for-profit organisation of game fishermen promoting awareness and conservation of grayling as a wild fish.

IFM (INSTITUTE OF FISHERIES MANAGEMENT),
ifm.org.uk
An organisation dedicated to the advancement of sustainable fisheries management across the British Isles.

RIVERFLY PARTNERSHIP,
riverflies.org
A network of organisations working together to protect the water quality of rivers, further the understanding of river fly populations and actively conserve river fly habitats.

RIVERS TRUST,
theriverstrust.org
An umbrella organisation with 65 member Trusts across the British Isles. It works with a large array of groups to help conserve and protect river habitats for both people and wildlife.

RSPB, rspb.org.uk
A charity for the conservation of birds and nature.

SURFERS AGAINST SEWAGE, sas.org.uk
A grassroots environmental charity that campaigns to protect the ocean.

WILD TROUT TRUST,
wildtrout.org
A conservation charity that focuses on practical work to improve habitat for trout across the UK and Ireland.

WILDFISH, wildfish.org
The only independent charity in the UK campaigning for wild fish and their environment. It works to diminish the key threats to wild fish, including open-net salmon farming, pollution and over-abstraction.

WILDFOWL AND WETLANDS TRUST,
wwt.org.uk
A charity dedicated to saving wetlands and their wildlife.

WILDLIFE TRUSTS,
wildlifetrusts.org
There are 46 individual Wildlife Trusts, each of which is a place-based independent charity dedicated to making a positive difference to wildlife and future generations.

WINDRUSH WASP,
windrushwasp.org
Collects and analyses information on water quality and sewage discharges in the Windrush valley.

Acknowledgements

I would first like to thank the team at Bloomsbury – Jim, Alice, Laura and the rest – for giving me the opportunity to write this book as for years I've wanted to write about the subject of rivers, something I hold so very dear to my heart. I originally pitched two books to Jim and I nearly had a heart attack when he commissioned both of them!

The team at WildFish, as always, have been a fantastic source of information for this book so thanks to Nick, Immy and Janina. Emma Brisdion at the Rivers Trust has also been really helpful.

I'd also like to thank, in no particular order, Ashley Smith, Josh Jaggard, Neil Philips, Josh Pickett, Jeremy Wade, Mark Owens, Pete Cooper, Ellie Mitchell, Kevin Murphy, Amanda Ward, Paul Russon, Celtic Rewilding, Ben Hollington, Billy Heaney and most importantly my two dachshunds Pepper and Rosie!

My wife Emma, as always, shows me incredible support and helps proofread my mad ramblings. To my Grandad John who encouraged and nursed my love of the outdoors from before I can remember: this book is for you.

Photo Credits

Key: RSPB = rspb-images.com; AL = Alamy; G = Getty; SS = Shutterstock; JP = Jack Perks

Front cover t Drew Buckley/RSPB; **Back cover** t JP, m JP, b JP; **1** Julian Gizzard/SS; **2–3** Nicola Pulham/SS; **4** JP; **6** JP; **7** Leanne Kelman; **8–9** Denis Chapman/AL; **10** JP; **11** Freya Connolly/The River Trust; **12** t JP, b Radenbow/SS; **13** Nick Upton/RSPB; **15** Cotswolds Photo Library Creative/AL; **16** Stuart Crump Impressions/AL; **17** Simon Whaley/AL; **18** Malkin Photography/AL; **19** t Erik Karits/SS, b JP; **20** tl JP, tr JP, b JP; **21** t JP, b JP; **22** t JP, b JP; **23** t JP, b JP; **24–25** lisa plant/AL; **26** Paul Hobson/Nature Picture Library; **27** Wozzie/SS; **28** Josh Jaggard; **29** JP; **30** JP; **31** Photos by R A Kearton/G; **32** JP; **33** JP; **34** JP; **35** t JP, b JP; **36** t JP, b JP; **37** t JP, b JP; **38** t JP, b Genevieve Leaper/RSPB; **39** t JP, b JP; **40–41** Alexey Fedorenko/AL; **42** JP; **43** t JP, b JP; **44** t JP; **45** JP; **46** Lucy M Ryan/SS; **47** John Davidson Photos/AL; **48** stocker1970/SS; **49** Billy Stock/SS; **50** JP; **51** t Josh Jaggard, b imageBROKER.com/AL; **52** t JP, b JP; **53** t JP, b JP; **54** t imageBROKER/Ottfried Schreiter/G, b JP; **55** t JP, b JP; **56–57** David Chapman/AL; **58** Simon Collins/SS; **59** t JP, b JP; **60** t JP, b Billy Heaney; **61** JP; **62** Josh Jaggard; **63** JP; **64** David Chapman/AL; **65** Nigel Jarvis/SS; **66** Jean Morrison/SS; **67** t JP, b Neil Phillips; **68** t Erni/SS, b JP; **69** t Josh Jaggard, b Neil Phillips; **70** t JP, b Josh Jaggard; **71** t JP, b JP; **72–73** stocker1970/SS; **74** JP; **75** t Nick Turner/AL, b JP; **76** David Norton/RSPB; **77** M G Photography/SS; **78** veryan dale/AL; **79** JP; **80** JP; **81** Neil Mitchell/SS; **82** Gerry McLaughlin/AL; **83** t Nature Picture Library/AL, b JP; **84** t JP, b JP; **85** t JP, b JP; **86** t JP, b Nature Picture Library/AL; **87** t JP, b JP; **88–89** Tony Martin Long/SS; **90** Juice Flair/SS; **91** JP; **92** Martin Hibberd/SS; **93** Phil Cutt/RSPB; **94** Danny Green/RSPB; **95** Josh Harrison/AL; **96** Jo Jones/SS; **97** Robert Harding Video/SS; **98** Mike Powles/G; **99** t JP, b JP; **100** t JP, b Neil Phillips; **101** t JP, b JP; **102** t JP, b Peter Turner Photography/SS; **103** t Kabar/SS, b Neil Phillips; **104–105** Thomas Marchhart/SS; **106–107** Simon Booth/SS; **108** JP; **109** Caia Image/G; **110** Pajor Pawel/SS; **111** JP; **112** Stephen Butler/SS; **113** nikonpete/SS; **114** JP; **115** t JP, b Josh Jaggard; **116** t JP, b JP; **117** t JP, b JP; **118** t JP, b JP; **119** t JP, b JP; **120–121** Darren Galpin/AL; **122** Voinalovych Mykola/SS; **123** JP; **124** JP; **125** JP; **126** JP; **127** MagicBones/SS; **128** t Kxba.k5/SS, b JP; **129** JP; **130** Tupungato/SS; **131** t JP, b JP; **132** t JP, b JP; **133** t JP, b JP; **134** t JP, b JP; **135** t Beautiful landscape/SS, b JP; **136–137** JP; **138** JP; **139** t JP, b Josh Jaggard; **140** t JP, b JP; **141** JP; **142** JP; **143** JP; **144** JP; **145** JP; **146** dnaveh/SS; **147** t JP, b JP; **148** t JP, b JP; **149** t JP, b JP; **150** t David Whitaker/AL, b JP; **151** t JP, b JP; **152–153** JP; **154** Josh Jaggard; **155** JP; **156** t JP, b Nicola Pulham/SS; **157** JP; **158** JP; **159** JP; **160** David Dennis/SS; **161** Martin Bache/AL; **162** t JP, b JP; **163** t JP, b JP; **164** t Neil Phillips, b JP; **165** t JP, b Josh Jaggard; **166** t AGAMI Photo Agency/AL, b JP; **167** t JP, b Tom Meaker/SS; **169** John Eccles/AL; **170** Nuttawut Uttamaharad/SS; **171** Tony Martin Long/SS; **172** JP.

Index

abstraction 91–2
Aire, River 120–1
aquariums, river 62
aquatic plant collecting 157
aquifers 11
art, outdoor 157
Attenborough Nature Reserve 63
Avon, River (Bristol) 49, 171; (Hampshire) 92

barbel 52
barriers, migration 42–3, 84
bat detecting 94
bearded tit 71
beautiful demoiselle 103
beaver, European 42, 53, 139, 143
birdwatching 29
bitterling, European 55
bittern 69
black poplar 51
bloody red mysid 107
boat rides 110
bridges, packhorse 6
brook lamprey 36
brown rat 131
brown trout 4, 36, 90, 92
buffers, riverside 58–9
bullhead 20
burbot 42, 68
butterbur 22

caddisfly 23
camera traps 60, 142
canals 104–19
cattle damage 27–8
chalk streams 88–103, 127
charr, Arctic 147
chub 132
chytrid fungus 156
citizen science 124–5
Clyde, River 18
Conwy estuary 82
Cothi, River 34
crabbing 77–8
Cromford Canal 111, 116

crucian 163
cuckoo 100
curlew 21
cycling 109–10

Daubenton's bat 166
Dee, River (Scottish) 146
Demon shrimp 132
Derwent, River 5, 31
dipper 38
dipping, river 13, 62
dog flea treatments 12
dog walking 125–6
Don, River 5, 30, 130
Donna Nook 79, 85
dragonfly-spotting 158
Driffield Beck 95
droppings 43–4
Dyfi, River 64

eel, European 76, 84
eel grass 86
elvermen 76
Erewash Canal 106–7, 111
Erewash, River 63
estuaries 72–87

farm ponds 159
Findhorn, River 138
fish eggs on duck's feet 155–6
fishing 44–5
flat-headed mayflies 151
flea treatments 12
floods 138–9
flounder 87
flowering rush 167
footprint trapping 142
foraging 122–3
forever chemicals 124
frog, common 152, 153, 156

gammarid shrimps 132
giant hogweed 54
glacial melt 10
Glaven, River 28–9, 98

glossary of river terms 172
golden-ringed dragonfly 23
golden weeping willow 102
goldeneye 149
goosander 150
Grand Union Canal 112
Grantham Canal 114
grass snake 135
grayling 37
great crested grebe 71
great crested newt 156, 164
great silver water beetle 164
greater bladderwort 165
grey heron 55
grey seal 79, 85
grey wagtail 22
gudgeon 115

Ham Wall 65
hidden rivers 123
hides 76
Himalayan balsam 134
horsefly 67

Insh Marshes 66
invasive species 107–9

keepers, river 91
Kennall, River 24–5, 32
Kennet, River 8–9, 88–9
kingfisher 131

large-grooved diving beetle 155
Lathkill, River 31, 92
Leeds and Liverpool Canal 113
Leighton Moss 56–7
lesser water boatman 26
litter 75–6, 106–7
little grebe 116
Llangollen Canal 104–5

mallard 133
mandarin duck 35
map of British rivers 7
mare's tail 103

marsh marigold 118
marsh samphire 85
Mawddach estuary 72–3
mayfly, common 99
meanings of river names 170
Mersey, River 106
mink, American 117, 149
mitten crab 87
moor frog 42
moth trapping 93
mud 74
mudlarking 76–7
mute swan 115

narrow-clawed crayfish 119
natterjack toad 156, 162
Nethy, River 33
Nidd, River 170
night visits 94
Norfolk hawker 165
number of British rivers 4

orange-striped stonefly 151
organisations 173
osprey 83
otter 43, 44, 51, 60, 94, 142
oxbow lakes 160
oystercatcher 86

paddling 46
palmate newt 19
pearl mussel 148
perch, European 117
photography, wildlife 61–2
pike 52
pingos 161
pitfall trapping 93
pollution, river 5, 50, 58, 133;
   see also flea treatments;
   forever chemicals; litter and
   road run-off
pond turtle, European 67
ponds 152–67
pool frog 156, 163
pubs, riverside 168–9
purple loosestrife 54
purple saxifrage 150

quicksand 74

raft spider 167
ragged robin 101
rainbow trout 92
ramshorn snail 134
reed, common 69
regional river terms 171
re-meandering 28–9, 154
rewilding 42
Ribble, River 47
roach 99
road run-off 123–4

salmon, Atlantic 27, 33, 96, 141,
   148
salmon farming 140
scarlet elf cup 39
sea lamprey 101
seed and stone collecting 30
Severn, River 17, 75, 76
signal crayfish 102
silver-washed fritillary 59
smelt 84
snipe 39
Snizort, River 136–7
snorkelling 141–2
Solway Firth 81
sources 8–23; see also under
   featured rivers
spate rivers, Scottish 136–51
Spey, River 144
sphagnum moss 11, 138
starry smooth-hound 83
starwort 38
stepping stones 12–13
Stiffkey, River 91
stocking, fish 92
stone loach 20
Stour, River 108, 124, 133
straightening rivers 90–1
swallowtail butterfly 70

tadpole shrimp 162
Taff, River 129
Tay, River 143
temporary ponds 162

Test, River 96
Thames estuary 80
Thames, River 11, 15, 40–1, 76–7,
   97, 127, 167
three-spined stickleback 133
tick, castor bean 19
tidal bores 74–5
tides 74–5
toad, common 20
Trent, River 5, 16, 59, 63
tributaries 11; see also under
   featured rivers
Tweed, River 145
Tyne, River 128

urban rivers 120–35

viewing windows 44
vocalisations, audibility of 26, 38

walks 14; see also dog walking
Wandle, River 127
water crowfoot, common 100
water deer, Chinese 68
water forget-me-not 37
water immersion, wildlife
   adaptations for 59–60
water mint 70
water rail 166
water scorpion 53
water shrew 21
water vole 117
waterfalls 139–40
Wensum, River 48
white-clawed crayfish 35
white-tailed eagle 147
Windrush, River 14, 97
woody debris 139
Wye, River (Derbyshire) 31;
   (Herefordshire) 2–3, 50

yellow flag iris 116
yellow waterlily 135
Ynys-hir 64

zander 118
zebra mussel 119